STARGÅTE
SG·1 ™

THE ILLUSTRATED COMPANION
SEASONS 3 AND 4

STARGATE SG-1: THE ILLUSTRATED COMPANION SEASONS 3 AND 4

1 84023 355 9

Published by
Titan Books
A division of
Titan Publishing Group Ltd
144 Southwark St
London
SE1 0UP

First edition April 2002
2 4 6 8 10 9 7 5 3 1

DEDICATION
As always, this book is dedicated to Philip, Kerry and my SG one, Stuart.

ACKNOWLEDGEMENTS
For dedication above and beyond the call of duty, my thanks go to all of the brilliant people involved in the production of *Stargate SG-1*. Whether cast, crew or catering, I am truly touched by their unfailing enthusiasm towards this series of books, and their willingness to answer all my queries at a moment's notice even when I pester them during their well-earned hiatus. Big hugs go to Lena Alami at Sky One for sending me *SG-1* tapes and loads of encouragement; the same goes for JD Downs at MGM. Extra special thanks are due to Adam Newell and Jo Boylett at Titan who didn't scream once when I told them my computer had crashed and burned, taking two thirds of this book with it. Those two have nerves of steel. And thank you to Richard Pasco, for his kind contribution. Once again, the biggest bouquet has to go to Mrs Cowan, publicist extraordinaire. Kim — you're simply the best!
—Thomasina Gibson

Titan Books would also like to thank Charlie Clementson, Kobie Jackson and James Leland at MGM for their continuing help. Thanks again to Richard Pasco, for the pictures from *Gatecon* 2001.

Did you enjoy this book? We love to hear from our readers. Please e-mail us at:
readerfeedback@titanemail.com or write to Reader Feedback at the above address. To subscribe to our regular newsletter for up-to-the-minute news, great offers and competitions, email: **titan-news@titanemail.com**

Titan Books' film and TV range are available from all good bookshops or direct from our mail order service. For a free catalogue or to order, phone **01536 764646** with your credit card details, or write to **Titan Books Mail Order, AASM Ltd, Unit 6, Pipewell Industrial Estate, Desborough, Northants, NN14 2SW**. Please quote reference SG/C2.

A CIP catalogue record for this title is available from the British Library.

Printed and bound in Great Britain by MPG, Bodmin, Cornwall.

STARGÅTE
SG·1™

THE ILLUSTRATED COMPANION
SEASONS 3 AND 4

Thomasina Gibson

Stargate SG-1 developed for television by
Brad Wright & Jonathan Glassner

TITAN BOOKS

Contents

When Thomasina asked me to write the Foreword for her book *Stargate SG-1: The Illustrated Companion Seasons 3 and 4*, I thought to myself, wow… that's a really long title. Then, I was flattered and honoured by the invitation, but then I found out it was volume two, a slight setback. Which is okay, until I thought about the fact that I had never written a Foreword before, and that I had never even read one because I always assume the book really starts with chapter one. So, now, I find myself in this peculiar situation of having to write something beyond this sentence. Then it dawned on me that this situation was in fact no different than any seed or springboard to science fiction. So I'll start this Foreword by going backwards.

In October 1996, I got a phone call from John Symes, the president of MGM Television. John and I had spent eight years together at Paramount. He was senior vice president of television and I was producing the *MacGyver* television series. John asked me what Rick (Dean Anderson) and I were up to these days. He knew Rick and I were partners in a production company called the Gekko Film Corp.

I told him that we had just finished a pilot for CBS called *Firehouse*, with Tom Fontana (*Homicide* and *OZ*), that didn't get picked up. So John, probably sensing easy prey, told me about this title and concept MGM had for a series based on the feature *Stargate*. The pitch was pretty good, and then I watched the film, but O'Neil didn't seem to be the type of character that I thought Rick would be interested in playing week after week. Then John said he would give us a 'forty-four' (a forty-four-episode commitment). I told John I would talk to Rick, and Rick agreed to a creative meeting to talk about his ideas and concerns.

So a meeting was set up with Brad Wright and Jonathan Glassner, the writer/executive producer team that we would partner with to produce the two-hour première and series. We talked about everything, deals were made (someday they'll be signed) and we were off to Vancouver, British Columbia to start pre-production. The challenge was to assemble the most talented film-makers in all creative departments, production design, camera, visual effects, etc, to help guarantee that our vision would make it to the screen. Richard Hudolin, the award-winning production designer, was already on board. We hired cinematographer Peter Woeste, whom Rick and I had worked with on *MacGyver*. Peter had just been nominated for an ASC award for his remake of *In Cold Blood*. It was beautifully shot,

and Peter is very tall, so he got the job. The script was rewritten for Rick's sensibilities, the sets and Stargate were built, the costumes were made, visual effects had done nothing, so we were obviously ready to start filming.

Above: Michael Greenburg with Richard Dean Anderson.

Day One, 19 February 1997. It rained so hard the raindrops were bouncing off the ground and two feet into the air. We were in dense forest so it got dark quickly. We ended up filming only one useable shot. Today, as I write this, it's 11 April 2001, and we're still here, now filming our 94th episode. I'm sitting with Amanda Tapping, reading this to her to make sure it's funny enough to ensure that there is still someone reading. Or, if you're like me, you've skipped the Foreword and have already started with chapter one, which means none of this really matters.

Michael Greenburg
Executive Producer *Stargate SG-1*

Continuing the Cycle

Jayne Dearsley

"Stargate SG-1 is the kind of show that you watch with an expectant half-smile on your face. This willingness to play with humour gives *Stargate* a more human side."

Within weeks of *Stargate SG-1* first appearing on screen, it became obvious to MGM and Showtime that they had, if you'll pardon the expression, a stellar hit on their hands. Broadcasters in countries outside the US and Canada, including Sky Television in the UK, were receiving such positive feedback that *Stargate SG-1*'s forty-four episode, two season commitment was expanded to double that amount. Already well into the swing of things, the running of the show developed from the initial 'teething problems' stage experienced by any new series, into what the cast and crew refer to as "a well-oiled machine." Although very much the result of a concerted team operation, the buck finally has to stop with someone, and the man responsible for keeping the aforementioned machine running smoothly is producer N. (for Norman) John Smith. "It is really down to all of us involved in the process," he modestly insists, "but basically it starts with Brad [Wright], the writers and myself. They come up with a story, and though it's my job to keep an eye on the finances, I tell them to concentrate on the script and not to write with a calculator or an adding machine on their mind because, if they do, all their creative powers will be diverted away."

Smith continues, "Inevitably, as executive producer, Brad always keeps the budget in mind when he's writing anyway, as does Robert Cooper because they know that if, for example, they write a scene where the good guys come blasting around the corner and the world blows up, sending debris everywhere — well — we can't afford to do that every week!" Chuckling Smith admits, "However, we can afford to do *some* things, so what we generally do is, as the script develops, actually write expensive sequences like that even bigger than is necessary, so that we can pull back if we need to. It's a lot easier to do that than the other way around, trying to make something bigger when we find we've got some cash unaccounted for."

Describing the process of how the sums work, Smith explains, "What we have at our disposal each season in monetary terms is twenty-two times the budget for each episode, which means we're responsible for bringing the production in on schedule without going over

that budget. Now the nature of the beast is that some episodes are bound to cost more, whilst some needn't cost so much, so the entire production team collaborates at the onset of each season to ensure that we keep the production values high, but stop costs from running away from us. At the start of each new year, we'll get some scripts and I'll look at them and figure — well — the first three are going to be way over, but the next couple are going to be under, and we'll balance the whole thing off. It's my job to get as much production value as possible, and ideally be just $1 under budget at the end of the year."

Above: Concept drawing of Hathor's planet from 'Into the Fire'.

Executive producer Richard Dean Anderson states, "John Smith is one of the best producers I've had the pleasure of working with. Although he has the dubious title of the man you love to hate, because he's the one who tells you there isn't enough money in the pot or the time available to do all the cool things you really want to do, John is brilliant at what he does, and that means the machinery of making this show is so well oiled that it almost runs itself."

Modest to a fault, Smith's reply to that is, "When you work with guys like we have on *Stargate SG-1* the job is very easy, because we're all working to the same goal. I've worked for other executive producers and production companies that aren't that 'together'. I've seen situations where the executive producers have tried to pull the wool over the eyes of the production company, and are determined not to be responsible to the budget." Smith's experience has taught him, "The bigger you can make the show, the more chance you have of good ratings, and the more chance you have of succeeding in your own personal career, but there has to be a bit of give and take. You have an obligation to the production company that hired you to do a specific job. They give you the money to spend judiciously, and if you do your job right you get all the pieces together and make everybody happy. It's a constant juggling act but one which I thoroughly enjoy."

Having seen the project up and running, *Stargate*'s co-creator Jonathan Glassner was extremely happy with the way the show was progressing. "We'd come through seasons one and two," he recalls. "The first half was basically spent trying to figure out what we wanted *Stargate SG-1* to be, and by season two we were very much on track for what we wanted to do. We blasted into season three with a lot of confidence, knowing that we had another couple of years to really expand the franchise. Plus, we were kind of on auto-pilot production wise. From an executive producer's point of view, Brad and I knew that everybody from the production designers to the guys who built the sets understood exactly what to do and what was expected of them. We knew we had a solid cast of compelling characters and strong actors. By season three we'd kind of hit our stride and there weren't that many changes in terms of personnel — except for me. Having helped get all of the above in place, I made a personal life decision to do what I'd meant to do even before getting involved with *Stargate*, and moved back to Los Angeles."

Glassner explains, "I'd already spent a lot of time in Vancouver doing *The Outer Limits* and was originally only meant to be there for a year. Then MGM kept offering me these carrots to stay — one of which was *Stargate*, the other was the prospect of working with Brad Wright on another show. When we struck the deal it was on the proviso that I gave the show three years, and I stuck to my end of the bargain. However, our home and family were down in LA and I had kept promising my wife that we'd only stay in Vancouver for 'one more year'. After several years of 'just one more year', we had reached decision time. We had had a baby in Vancouver, we'd made new friends, we were going to have to make the full commitment and emigrate to Canada, or return home." Glassner admits that it was very hard leaving

Above: SG-1 consider their next 'Gate jump.

the fold and moving to pastures new, but says, "I knew I was leaving my other 'baby' in extremely good hands." Brad Wright, Glassner's co-creator adds, "We all supported Jonathan's decision, and the rest of us had a little bit of a shift round, brought in new members to our writing team and embarked on a whole new round of challenges. We continued to blend great stories with spectacular visual effects and the tongue-in-cheek humour that prevents our show from taking itself too seriously, but moved ahead with renewed energy."

A major contributor to the continuing success of *Stargate SG-1* is 'new' co-executive producer Robert C. Cooper, who had actually been an integral part of the team since the show's inception: "I came on board very early on, and was the show's executive story editor. I was meant to be here on a sort of temporary basis, but ended up staying!" Brad Wright has said many times that, "Robert Cooper is in many ways the heart and soul of *Stargate*. He's written the most episodes, come up with the most ideas, and grown to fill Jonathan's shoes." John Smith echoes the sentiment: "Robert is a pretty prolific writer, which is just as well for us, because without him we would have suffered quite a bit during the early years. Some of our junior writers at that

Above: Closing the lid on Hammond and Teal'c — behind the scenes on 'Into the Fire'.

time would pitch ideas, but it almost came to the point where Jonathan, Brad and Robert spent so much time telling the writers how to get the storyline across that they might as well have written it themselves. Robert really had his work cut out as story editor at that time."

Smith confirms that writers Joseph Mallozzi and Paul Mullie were a timely addition to the staff: "These guys are terrific. They've got tons of energy. Then Peter DeLuise came on board and though he is not a polished writer, he also has tons of energy and a million ideas. So all of a sudden it wasn't just Brad, Jonathan and Robert pitching ideas to the other writers. We were on a roll, because Paul and Joe in particular would turn in scripts that just needed a couple of minor changes here and there, and away we'd go."

According to Brad Wright, Messrs Mullie and Mallozzi are "the new blood that *Stargate SG-1* needed, and I can't praise them enough for their ability to take a story that we work out together in a room, and come back a couple of days later with a knockout script." As for Peter DeLuise, Wright says, "I wasn't joking when I said I gave him the job of creative consultant just to get him out of my office! The man was living and breathing everything *Stargate* and when you have

someone willing to do that, it's important to invest in them and reward them for their intensity and for their embracing of the universe you are attempting to create."

Above: Director Peter DeLuise tries to persuade RDA to read the script.

Another man who continues to guide *Stargate SG-1* towards a fifth and sixth season is executive producer Michael Greenburg. Part of the team whose task is to assume overall responsibility for everything pertaining to the show, Greenburg is the man who is there all day, every day as 'on set' producer: "All the executive producers wear several hats, for instance Rick also acts and edits, Brad and Robert handle the scripts, and I oversee the actual production in terms of taking care of the day-to-day issues that occur at any given moment during the shoot." Brushing aside any suggestion that it has to be one of the most arduous jobs going, the softly-spoken Greenburg smiles, "Not at all. We have an incredibly flexible and collaborative group of people pulling together. Consequently it's not hard at all." As *Stargate SG-1* breezes towards its fifth year, Greenburg is as enthusiastic about the show as he was on day one: "We've still got lots of surprises to come. My advice is to expect the unexpected and you won't be disappointed." ⋏

Into the Fire

Regular Cast: Richard Dean Anderson (Colonel Jack O'Neill), Michael Shanks (Dr Daniel Jackson), Amanda Tapping (Captain Samantha Carter), Christopher Judge (Teal'c), Don S. Davis (General Hammond), Teryl Rothery (Dr Janet Fraiser)

Written by: Brad Wright
Directed by: Martin Wood

Guest cast: Tony Amendola (Bra'tac), Suanne Braun (Hathor), Tom Butler (Major General Trofsky), Colin Cunningham (Major Davis), Samantha Ferris (Dr Raully), Gary Jones (Technician)

mprisoned on the psychotic Hathor's planet, Daniel and Carter are forced to watch O'Neill become a host for the Goa'uld queen's first mate. Back on Earth, and with all other efforts to rescue SG-1 thwarted, General Hammond risks court martial by jumping through the gate to mount an attempt of his own. Teal'c, meanwhile, returns to Chulak and tries to raise a Jaffa army against the Goa'uld. Unaware that a Tok'ra spy has managed to save O'Neill from several lifetimes with 'junior' by putting him in a cryogenic chamber, Teal'c and Hammond fire up an ancient Death Glider and blast through the Stargate to literally snatch their comrades from the jaws of death…

O'Neill to Jaffa warriors

"Our Beloved Hathor is dead. Well, let's face it! She's a former Queen."

"What I *really* liked in that episode," begins director Martin Wood, "was being able to use the 'real' Cheyenne Mountain base set, and then change it just enough so we got a feel of 'is this real or isn't it?' for Hathor's 'duplicate' base. One of the things I always thought was so cool about the base set was that it had this huge wall that could roll aside, with an equally huge green screen behind it. I'd always wanted to use it, but we'd never had the chance. So when Robert Cooper said to me, 'They go in and push a button and the wall starts to move,' I was ecstatic! Remember the scene where they find the power switch to the generator for the 'false' base? That was such a great shot. O'Neill walks into the Gateroom, goes over to a box that's never been there before and says, 'This is new…' Then he pulls the lever and the wall moves aside — I thought it was one of the coolest things I'd ever seen! A lot of fans have said the same thing. Some of them actually thought we'd built a new set just for Hathor to work in, but it was just the same old base."

The effervescent Mr Wood also reveals that the episode saw the beginning of the force shield that was to play such a huge part in the season four story 'Upgrades'. "We were never really sure how to get that thing working but in 'Into the Fire', when we were tapping on it and touching the shield, it was the kind of effect that gave visual effects supervisor James Tichenor a headache. Trying to get this interactive light on the cast, and make it look like there was something between the actors, was a major operation. But one of the things I love most about this show are the practical discussions that we get into over these things."

Above: Hammond and Teal'c prepare to thread the needle — Into the Fire.

Giving insight into the goings-on at the daily production meetings, Wood says there are two people who are masters of throwing spanners into the works, who won't let any nebulous idea or vague concept get through unchallenged — executive producer Michael Greenburg and director of photography Jim Menard: "They do it quite simply because some things don't make sense, and our audience is going to tell us that." Chuckling, Wood insists, "In any one meeting you can count on Jim Menard to go, 'But that's impossible!' Then he'll mumble some way of explaining it, and we'll all respond, 'Yes, Jim, but if we do that, the script will end after five pages.' Eventually we all do get our heads round the problem, so that whatever Jim or Michael bring up, we can work around it." ⅄

Seth

Written by: Jonathan Glassner Directed by: William Corcoran	Guest Cast: Carmen Argenziano (Jacob Carter/ Selmak), Robert Duncan (Seth), Mitchell Kosterman (Special Agent James Hamner), Stuart O'Connell (Tommy Levinson)

O'Neill, Carter and Daniel swap their airforce fatigues for white robes and sandals in order to help Carter's father, Jacob, flush a Goa'uld System Lord from hiding. Ensconced deep within a remote complex in Washington State, Seth has used the lure of alternative religious beliefs, combined with the same biological compound used by Hathor, to brainwash a long line of followers and maintain a powerful presence on Earth for thousands of years. With agents from the ATF and a frantic father ready to storm the heavily armed fortress at any moment, SG-1 must resort to desperate measures to prevent both Seth's escape and the inevitable bloodshed of his disciples.

> **Daniel to O'Neill**
>
> "The men usually became eunuchs."
>
> "Eunuchs! As in snippitty doo-dahs?"

Jonathan Glassner opens by saying, "As writers, one of the things we wanted to do as much as we could was to figure out stories we could do on Earth, because as we were going to other planets every week, doing a show on our own planet was actually like a breath of fresh air. The idea for 'Seth' occurred when I was watching a documentary about David Koresh. I thought, 'What if one of these modern cult leaders actually had powers, or the technology to make it look as though he had powers? How far would he be able to go with that?' Then it occurred to me that as Goa'ulds were able to jump from body to body, they could live for a very long time. Therefore, who's to say that one of them wasn't still around and masquerading as a cult figure? So Seth was sort of a David Koresh metaphor."

Choosing the actor to play the villainous Seth was plain sailing as far as Glassner was concerned: "The curse of casting a bad guy is that everyone always comes in virtually twirling a moustache, you know, your typical bad guy. But Robert Duncan walked in the room and before he even got into character we all thought he looked kinda scary. We just told him to be himself and he pulled it off." Another coup was the choice of venue. Says Glassner: "The place we used as the complex was

Above: Sitting pretty
— Seth on his throne.

really this neat old mansion that is now a national landmark. It gets used for official functions, for example, former US President Clinton and one of the Russian leaders met there. It was a very cool location."

Whilst the setting may have been ideal, Amanda Tapping was less than impressed with some aspects of the episode, particularly the furniture: "We just thought it was insane that there was this really powerful, freakin' System Lord and thousands of years later he's got a following of twelve people and a throne encrusted with jewels!" Reining in her exasperation for a moment, she shrugs, "We thought the concept of the episode was really clever, but I personally feel he should have accomplished so much more than just garner a cult following and a chair." Dissolving into giggles, she snorts, "I mean, where the hell did he get that throne? Did he cart that with him, across the centuries, from Egypt and all through the Galaxy and back through the Stargate and down again? It's a honkin' big throne, c'mon!" Attempts to stem the flow by suggesting that perhaps it was his favourite chair, his comfy one, are met with total derision. "Well he should have picked up a nice comfortable little Chippendale. I'm sure that would have been a lot easier." Finishing with, "That's my thought," Ms Tapping finally simmers down. ⋋

Fair Game

Written by: Robert C. Cooper
Directed by: Martin Wood

Guest Cast: Michael David Simms (Secretary of Defence Arthur Simms), Ron Halder (Cronus), Jacqueline Samuda (Nirrti), Vince Crestejo (Yu)

Jack O'Neill's fishing trip is put on hold when his favourite Asgard, Thor, reveals an audacious plan to attack Earth. Offering to help negotiate a way to make Earth part of the protected planets treaty, the tiny alien insists that the irreverent Colonel, rather than the somewhat more diplomatic Daniel, represent the Earth at a meeting with three Goa'uld System Lords. The meeting does not go well, with O'Neill managing to offend the guests within seconds. Things take an even nastier turn when Cronus, the Goa'uld responsible for the death of Teal'c's father, is found badly beaten, with a slightly less battered Teal'c at his side. A revenge attack on Earth seems likely until Carter manages to use a Goa'uld healing device to restore Cronus to health, and Nirrti's true motivation becomes clear...

Daniel Jackson

"I'll see to the petty needs of the Goa'uld."

Director Martin Wood has a definite fondness for this episode. "That's where we meet Cronus, Nirrti and Yu," he grins. "It was one of those times where we cast people with the hope that maybe the story would turn into something else, perhaps another arc. In this case we tried it with the three System Lords. That in itself was a riot because when we were planning the characters it was like, 'OK! What gods are we going to go after this time?' So we began this raffle, and everybody threw in their three choices. After loads of discussion, we finally came up with three gods to fit the bill. Yu made us laugh a lot, because no-one could resist making jokes with the name. When Yu appeared in the story, we'd be like, 'So — what do you want to do?' and someone would crack, 'What do you mean, what do you

Nirrti and Yu

Nirrti is the Hindu goddess of darkness. A deceitful, destructive deity she uses her power of invisibility to wreak havoc wherever possible. Yu is not a god in the true sense, but the fact that he was supposed to have sprung from the body of a dragon gives him a certain mythical kudos.

Above: Three of a kind — Yu, Nirrti and Cronus.

want Yu to do? What is it you want Yu to do?' Even worse, if we had a gap in the story and needed a character to do something, some idiot would go, 'How about Yu?' and that would start us off again: 'How about Yu, the System Lord or how about me?'" How the days must have flown by…

According to the director, one of the worst culprits was Richard Dean Anderson. "He took it apart every time. The only time we got him to behave, if you could call it that, was when he had to do scenes with Thor. He loves working with that little guy; the scenes between Thor and O'Neill really were a riot to do," says Wood. "Rick had the best time. Each time he walked over to talk to Thor, the puppeteers would make him talk back, but with hilarious ad-libs. There are so many outtakes of Thor yelling things like, 'Dammit! What's my line?' My colleague, Andy Mikita, has some great outtakes where Thor turns round just before he goes on camera and leers, 'So, I went out with these babes…' and sets us all laughing again." Wood maintains that Adam Behr, the head puppeteer, is a very funny guy, and plays around with the Thor character every chance he gets. One of Wood's major regrets is that there are no crew outtake tapes in wider circulation. "I always print the outtakes, but we're not allowed to let a tape go out to fan conventions or wherever. It's a shame because *Stargate* is the funniest show I've ever worked on, and it just gets funnier every year." Å

Legacy

Written by: Tor Alexander Valenza
Directed by: Peter DeLuise

Guest Cast: Kevin McNulty (Dr Warner), Eric Schneider (Dr McKenzie), Michael Shanks (Machello)

D aniel Jackson is dressed in white again, but this time he's within the confines of a padded cell. On a routine mission which unearths a secret room housing the corpses of the Lindross — a Goa'uld group who challenged the superiority of the System Lords — Daniel is unknowingly infected with a device which was designed by Machello to kill Goa'uld. Consequently plagued with visions and hearing disembodied voices, he is diagnosed as the victim of schizophrenia and locked away for safe keeping. As Teal'c tries to restrain his distraught colleague, the bio-engineered parasite transfers to the Jaffa, with immediate and catastrophic results to his symbiote. When a tablet which Daniel believes could contain the information to cure this affliction is opened, Fraiser and O'Neill are infected too. It then becomes a race against time to prevent Teal'c's death and the deterioration of his friends' mental abilities.

O'Neill

"Let's put up a little sign at the bottom of the ramp saying, 'Gate travel may be hazardous to your health.'"

"That was the episode where Daniel Jackson had the Goa'uld killer in him," confirms director Peter DeLuise. "It was a great opportunity for Michael Shanks to do his thing. The episode was firmly focussed on him and the madness caused by Machello's invention. But you know what's a shame and ironic about the Goa'uld killer, is that we never fully investigated the potential of that. Those nine dead guys, those bodies (which we used many times subsequently, by the way), were freed from their symbiotes, and only died because they starved to death or dehydrated or something like that. So if we needed to find something to rid us of Goa'ulds — and many times we've gone, 'Oh, wouldn't it be great if we could remove this thing?' — I'm wondering why we haven't decided to re-use Machello's parasite. I mean, it only made Daniel Jackson and the others go crazy and wacky because they didn't have a symbiote in them…" It's clearly something we'll have to look out for in later episodes from the crazy and wacky Peter DeLuise.

Whilst congratulating all involved for acting their socks off, executive producer Jonathan Glassner was not happy with the final scenes:

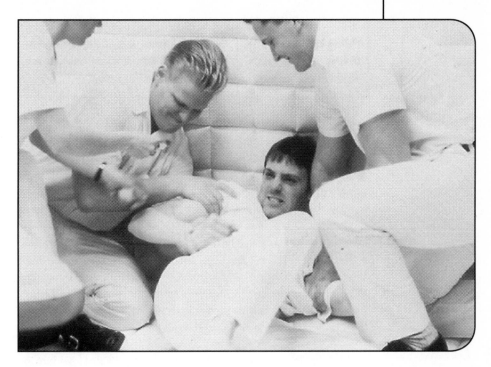

"When we looked at the cut of the last act, when O'Neill, Carter and Fraiser are locked in the science lab and dealing with the worms, we were really concerned about what we were going to do, because we thought it was the most boring thing we'd ever seen! The trouble was, everything that was left in the cut was totally necessary for the story and the exposition, so we couldn't lose any of it. In desperation, we called the composer, Kevin Kliner, and said, 'Help us on this.' He came back with the music that transformed the scene to completely on-the-edge-of-your-seat riveting. To me that is the best example of what music can do for a TV show. One day, I'm going to take that example and use it in a class for film students."

Above: Daniel succumbs to Machello madness.

The madness may have caused a few wobbly moments in some quarters but it proved no problem at all for Richard Dean Anderson. Asked how difficult it was to portray a man going quietly mad he replies, with just a trace of a twinkle in his eye, "I have no trouble whatsoever portraying a guy going mad — quietly mad, loudly mad, any sort of mad, primarily because I've been practising that my entire life. I've been, I think, going quietly mad for a very long time. I started when I was a very small boy. So I wasn't taxed at all because I've had lots of practice." ᛉ

Learning Curve

Written by: Heather E. Ash	Guest Cast: Andrew Airlie (Kalan), Brittney Irvin
Directed by: Martin Wood	(Merrin), Lachlan Murdoch (Tomin), Stephanie Shea
	(Solen), Diane Stapley (Mrs Struble)

I t's a return to the days of the old schoolyard for Carter and then O'Neill when they discover that an eleven year-old from the planet Orban is smarter than your average girl. Whilst Daniel is busy sharing his archaeological skills with some willing students and Teal'c imparts his knowledge of the Goa'uld to an enthusiastic young pupil, Merrin travels to Earth and offers to teach Carter how to build a Naquadah reactor. Although fascinated by her grasp of advanced physics and technical drawing, Carter and O'Neill soon realise that a major component of Merrin's life is missing. Determined to show and explain how much fun 'play' can be, O'Neill sneaks the child off base and into a local school. The lessons she learns there prove to be infinitely valuable to all the people of Orban.

> **O'Neill**
>
> "Teal'c's eager on the inside."

Writer Heather E. Ash has this to share about her first foray into the *Stargate* universe: "This was the script that got me hired to join the full-time writing staff. My draft was distributed to the crew without a rewrite by Brad or Jonathan, which was a first for a freelance script (and the last time it happened for me)." Delighted to be hired in time to see her episode filmed, Ash says, "I was so impressed with both Rick [Dean Anderson] and Christopher Judge, and their interaction with the children. Especially the scene where Merrin leaves for the last time, and O'Neill is watching her go. I got teary watching it. The very final scene, where O'Neill colours with Merrin, was mostly ad-libbed."

Ash also owns up to a tiny personal indulgence: "Mrs Struble was named after Christine Struble, my second grade teacher whom I'm still friends with." Sadly, the writer's second indulgence was short-lived. "The idea for a portable Naquadah reactor was my creation and the prop itself was fantastic. It was a hollow shell of small, intricate pieces glued together, with a blue 'light sheet' inside, activated by a hidden switch. It was beautiful. I kept it in my office for a few months until the prop police made me give it back!"

Amanda Tapping reveals a fun moment for Carter and Merrin: "There's a scene where we are in the lab and get that energy wave off the

bomb. Well, without telling us, the crew had rigged up a bunch of vibrating devices onto the big metal desk. So when the energy wave took place and the bomb exploded, the table actually shook. The reaction you see on screen really is us going, 'Argh! My God!' I just love it when the crew do little things like that."

Above: Student and teacher: but which is which? Carter and Merrin discover together.

Tapping particularly enjoyed the episode, she says, "because of the moral dilemma it posed, as in, 'Do we have the right to get that involved in another people's way of life?' It's a question we ask often on *Stargate* but what I found poignant this time is that the children are essentially put out to pasture. What do you do with that? There's got to be more you can teach them. There is one part where Merrin insists she wants to have the nanocytes which make her so intelligent removed, which will effectively turn her into a vegetable, and I tell her that most of the best things in my life happened after I was fifteen. The line was originally written differently, but I changed it to include my personal observation as Amanda, and they kept it in. I loved the way that scene played." ⋏

Point of View

Story by: Jonathan Glassner, Brad Wright, Robert C. Cooper, Tor Alexander Valenza
Teleplay by: Jonathan Glassner and Brad Wright
Directed by: Peter DeLuise

Guest Cast: Jay Acovone (Major Charles Kawalsky), Peter Williams (Apophis), Ty Olsson (Jaffa #1), Shawn Reis (Jaffa #2), Tracy Westerholm (SF Guard)

The SGC are subjected to a two-for-one offer when a second Dr Carter, accompanied by a very live and kicking Major Kawalsky, slips through the quantum mirror (first seen in 'There But For the Grace of God') into Area 51. Identical to SG-1's Carter in every way except for her longer hairstyle and the fact that she's a civilian, the new Sam causes more than one double take when she reveals she was married to Jack O'Neill, before his demise at the hands of the Goa'uld. Gamely resisting all advances from 'Mrs' O'Neill, the Colonel works with the rest of SG-1 to help both Carters find a way to repel the marauding Goa'uld and return the visitors to their own reality.

O'Neill to Dr Carter

"How could you marry such a loser?"

"'Point of View' came about because we wanted the opportunity for Carter and O'Neill to kiss and had to figure out a way to do it," admits Jonathan Glassner. "In the original script, the alternative reality Carter was also an officer, but our Air Force advisors who approve such things refused to grant permission for that to go ahead. Their official stance was: 'Two military officers cannot kiss.' Even when I said, 'How do you know that's the rule in an alternate reality?' they said it didn't matter. So Brad Wright and I came up with the idea right there and then on the phone. We asked how it would be if one wasn't in the military, and they gave in and let us go with that."

Displaying his complete understanding of the female psyche, jovial Peter DeLuise shrugs off the complicated technical nature of the production and concentrates on the most difficult challenge, which was to deal with the issue of the twin Carters' coiffure: "As you know, hair, in production, is one of the bigger considerations for women, so when you do a twinning shot where half the shot is being done at a time, hair can cause some problems." In fuller detail he explains, "Amanda was required to do half of each scene with her photo double, go off and

change, then come back and do the next half. Her hair took about half an hour to change over because if she had the wig on, we'd do the first version and we would have to make her real hair from underneath the wig all fluffy — nice and presentable so she didn't have 'wig head'. The converse was also true. If she had a nice fluffy hairdo, then we had to crush it with the wig, make sure the bangs were dealt with and make sure it was not riding up so it looked as though she had a misshapen head!"

Above: It's Hammond and Teal'c, but not as we know them.

Thankfully, DeLuise excels in fields other than hairdressing. He is justifiably proud of pulling off the scene in the medical centre when Carter had to hold her own hand. "Usually you can't touch your other self without it looking fake," he admits. "But our audience is quite savvy and knows that if you take a really close look at that scene the seam is flawless, and that's because where her hands touch is not where the seam is. It's down near the elbow where the blanket is covering her up." So now we know. λ

Deadman's Switch

Written by: Robert C. Cooper
Directed by: Martin Wood

Guest Cast: Sam J. Jones (Aris Boch), Mark Holden (Korra)

A routine mission to planet PJ6-877 turns out to be more than a walk in the forest when SG-1 are ambushed and captured by intergalactic bounty hunter Aris Boch. Painfully addicted to a substance he can only get from the Goa'uld, Boch offers to trade the lives of SG-1 for that of a criminal named Kel'tar — so long as they assist in his capture. After an escape attempt goes awry, O'Neill, Daniel and Teal'c are forced to comply with Boch's wishes. When they realise the criminal is in fact Korra, a Tok'ra, and therefore an ally, SG-1 must find a way to convince their captor to do the right thing and let them go.

> **O'Neill**
>
> "We're exactly one zat gun short of actually having a zat gun."

Martin Wood struggles to stop laughing when reminiscing about 'Deadman's Switch': "For a start, it's the first one that doesn't actually have a Stargate in it, though nobody ever notices until we tell them. Michael Greenburg brought it up. He turned to us one day and said, 'You know what? There is no Stargate in this episode of *Stargate*. We should rename the show — *Stargate (or not)!*'" Kawoosh or no Kawoosh, Wood states, "Sam Jones was hilarious when we were shooting that episode. My favourite thing that happened was when we were filming some of Sam's dialogue and his line was something like, 'My wife and son were kidnapped!' and I said, 'Sam, you don't actually have a wife.' He looked at me and asked, 'What do you mean? I thought I did.' So I explained that it was just Aris Boch bluffing, and in the next scene we find out that he doesn't have a wife. So Sam went, 'OK — but how would you say this line?' I gave him a reading, which he repeated exactly, I shot it, and on we went. The whole episode was like that with him. I think Sam Jones really is an alien," Wood continues with a laugh. "He doesn't understand the rules and regulations of human life, so brought this alien character to life in a way that nobody else could."

Aside from the visiting alien, Wood's favourite part of the episode was when the bounty hunter's ship, his Teltac, climbs up over the rise: "I fought for that shot. I loved it so much. I took the idea from the movie *Blue Thunder*, when the helicopter is revealed. When I was a

kid I thought it was the coolest shot *ever*. It was so great to reveal something so vast that you can't hear until it's on top of you. I chose the location area with the ravine where we filmed specifically to do that shot. It
was such a thrill to put all the elements together, and James Tichenor
went all out with the visual effects and made that shot work. The next
shot, where the ship takes off from the ground and the wings come out
and the door closes, was accomplished by James's team using huge fans
to blow the dirt around and set the trees flapping. They were wonderful."

Wood's admiration extends to the skills displayed by actor
Christopher Judge: "When you see Teal'c throw the smoke bomb into
the cave, Chris turned around and the very first time he picked it up,
he threw it and it landed in the cave, exactly as it was supposed to.
Now, I can't throw that far when I'm standing up and looking, but
Chris was lying down and he just lobbed this thing. Nobody could
believe it went in. Sadly we couldn't use the shot because when he
opened up the smoke bomb he burned his thumb, and then ruined
the take by yelling some very unsavoury words!" ʎ

Above: Behold!
The bounty hunter
Aris Boch.

Demons

Written by: Carl Binder
Directed by: Peter DeLuise

Guest Cast: David McNally (Simon), Alan C. Peterson (Canon), Laura Mennell (Mary), Richard Morwich (Unas), John R. Taylor (Elder), Christopher Judge (Voice of the Unas)

Arriving at a medieval village, Daniel Jackson releases a young girl from the stake to which she is tied, whilst O'Neill's knowledge of childhood illnesses comes to the fore when he recognises that the marks on her body are chicken pox, rather than the manifestation of an evil presence. Less than impressed, the local Canon proclaims these actions are evil, and that SG-1 are agents of the Devil. With Teal'c subjected to numerous trials for witchcraft and the whole team offered up as sacrifices to the Unas that haunts the community, it's left to the very devout Simon to go against all he believes in order to free SG-1 and banish the demon forever.

Amanda Tapping remembers 'Demons' as being "pretty funny because Peter DeLuise, who makes everything fun, directed it. He had crew-members running through screaming, dressed up as villagers playing havoc. What I remember most, though, is the village set. It was phenomenal. I spent most of my time crawling around in corners looking at the painting and the construction detail! That was by far one of my favourite sets ever in terms of attention to detail. For example, you know how the villagers had those metal hooks that they chained us to? Well, there was actual rust going down the walls from the metal, and

> ### Teal'c to O'Neill
>
> "Have you not read the Bible, O'Neill?"
>
> "Not all of it. Actually, I'm listening to it on tape. Don't tell me how it ends."

The Original Hosts

Larger than your average human, stronger than an ox and as ferocious-looking as a wild beast, the mighty Unas were the original hosts of the Goa'uld. These once peaceful creatures became infected by the primordial snake-like parasites that inhabited the drinking water near the Unas's natural environment. Only by staying clear of the shores could they avoid the fate of being taken as a host. Unfortunately, many Unas quickly succumbed to the evil ones, and carried their symbiotes through the Stargate, allowing the Goa'uld to become the dominant force in the Galaxy.

Above: A medieval native takes the restraining order very seriously.

all sorts of other little touches like that. The set crew had moss growing up some of the walls, too — the sort of detail that you maybe don't see straight off when you're watching the episode, but if you see it up close and are acting in that kind of environment, it's just amazing."

Christopher Judge remembers his first reaction to the episode: "When I first read it, and got to the part where Teal'c gets thrown down into the water, I just wanted to make sure that it wasn't going to be *me* doing it!" Ignoring the fact that he was a professionally trained athlete, Judge whines, "You know, I'm not the strongest swimmer in the world, plus I knew that water would be freezing. So I was extremely happy that I had a stunt double for it. He certainly earned his money."

Sharing Tapping's fondness for Peter DeLuise, Judge says, "Peter directed it, so it was a hoot to do. Peter didn't tell the women who were watching over my body that I would be coming back to life. The shock on their faces was genuine, they were scared silly! It was the first time we had re-visited the Unas, and Alan Peterson who played the Canon went wonderfully over the top with his delivery, and had us all falling about." ⅄

Rules of Engagement

Written by: Terry Curtis Fox **Directed by:** William F. Gereghty	**Guest Cast:** Peter Williams (Apophis), Aaron Craven (Captain Kyle Rogers), Dion Johnstone (Captain Nelson), Jesse Moss (Lt J. Hibbard)

S tepping through the gate straight into a pitched battle between SG forces and a group of Jaffa, the members of SG-1 are literally stunned when their own side turns and fires on them. Waking inside a prison tent on what appears to be an army base, SG-1 discover a group of young men left stranded by their Jaffa leaders and still intent on fulfilling their standing orders, which were to practice non-lethal war games in readiness for the invasion of Earth. Duping the soldiers into believing that Teal'c is still Apophis's First Prime, sent with the rest of SG-1 to test the prowess of the Jaffa, seems to be the only way of persuading the troops to surrender and return to their homes.

Teal'c to Jaffa troops

"This is Colonel O'Neill. He is much loved by Apophis."

"One of the very best things about 'Rules of Engagement' was that it gave me a chance to return to my youth, and romp around like a kid again," chuckles Christopher Judge. "I really liked that episode. We had all these youngsters running around. We got to do a lot of fighting with Rick and that's his thing, rolling around in the mud and doing all that kind of action stuff. It was great to see him taking such an active part, and because *he* literally threw himself into it, so did everyone else. I remember one day when it was raining and we had to do a lot of running and diving in the dirt, which was now very sloppy mud, Rick and I just turned to each other and said, 'This is the best day we've had all season!'" Exaggerating slightly, Judge grins, "We were these two old guys who were now back to being kids again, so in that respect it was such a great episode. Getting to play soldiers, and winding up the costume

The Vo'cume

An essential piece of kit for any false god, or anyone else wishing to entertain the troops, this Goa'uld device can project a recorded audio/visual image. Able to reproduce the subject in larger-than-life Technicolor detail, it is most often used as a symbol of authority to issue orders to Jaffa from afar.

and make-up ladies because we were so filthy was *tremendous*." Publicist Kim Cowan can testify to the state they were in — she has photographic evidence pinned on the wall of her office. But, of course, that's classified!

Above: *Apophis's First Prime inspects the troops.*

Judge says the humorous banter between Teal'c and O'Neill carried on off-camera too. "We had a really good time when the cameras stopped rolling and kind of kept the Teal'c/O'Neill master/servant thing going. I think it's the only time Richard Dean Anderson served me lunch. Ah! Only kidding folks."

Very often the episode we see on television is a very different version to what was first proposed. "'Rules of Engagement' was a script that went through three incarnations," explains Brad Wright. "The first, written by Terry Curtis Fox, bears almost no resemblance to what was finally committed to film. Our story editor at the time, Tor Valenza, came up with a spin on Terry's story that finally made it work for me — which is the idea of young soldiers training to infiltrate the Tauri and being left behind. I then did a very heavy re-write on Tor's script and that's what we shot." ⋏

Forever in a Day

Written by: Jonathan Glassner
Directed by: Peter DeLuise

Guest Cast: Erick Avari (Kasuf), Vaitiare Bandera (Sha're/Ammonet), Jason Schombing (Robert Rothman)

T hings look fairly dire for the future of SG-1 when Teal'c makes the decision to kill Ammonet, the Goa'uld infesting Daniel's wife Sha're, rather than let her destroy the archaeologist. Unable to forgive Teal'c for his actions nor continue his quest through the Stargate without Sha're as his goal, Daniel rejects Teal'c's friendship, resigns from the Stargate programme and leaves to begin a new life far away from the SGC. However, the gods and Sha're still have plans in store which mean Daniel must overcome his grief and forgive Teal'c before he can go on to fulfil a promise.

Daniel Jackson

"The SGC may be the single most important endeavour for the future of Mankind."

Jonathan Glassner is very proud of this episode, and thinks it's his best script for the series: "The idea came out of a desire to finally wrap up the Sha're story. However, Sha're being out there was sort of Daniel Jackson's over-riding motivation to stay with SG-1, so we had to come up with a new goal. That's where the Harsesis child came in, which, giving credit to the proper person, was actually Robert Cooper's idea."

According to Glassner, all of the rituals involved in the burial rites for Sha're were the real thing — as far as the ancient scrolls are concerned: "They believed that if the soul was lighter than a feather it would go to Heaven, but if it wasn't it would go to the Underworld. The scales we used were based on a real one that was found on an archaeological dig, and when Daniel is reciting the burial rites, he's doing it as informed linguists think it would have been pronounced. Of course, no one really knows that for sure, but it was as close as we could get it."

'Forever in a Day' was one of Michael Shanks's favourites too: "It was an episode that marked the end of a continuing story line that was very significant to the character, and as such was a very emotional time for me. It was a lot of fun to play the sadness and to explore the torn nature of the decisions the character was making and to play, in a sense, the end of that character's arc." Shanks agrees with Wright that "the 'funeral' scene and the scenes in the apartment were wonderful. Those were rare, few and far between opportunities to go to personal places. The nature of *Stargate* being what it is, ie steeped in the science fiction

Above: Sha're and Daniel, alone at last.

mode, it was a treat to take Daniel on this deeply personal journey and have him pop up on the other side."

Though fun, the actor comments that the sometimes very personal nature of the episode took some getting used to: "It was done with my girlfriend at the time, Vaitiare Bandera, and it was one of those things that held a lot of personal angst, but the bedroom scene was completely natural because it felt like we were in a hotel room together, except there were all these people standing around with cameras. So it was, 'Guys? What are you doing in our room?' Vaitiare was very nervous, and stayed so professional and a little distant as a result. Whereas it was natural for us to cuddle in between takes in any other circumstance, she was much more reserved because she wasn't as comfortable with the crew as I was. It felt odd in my own mind because I kept thinking, 'This is us as we usually are. We do this all the time. Go film something interesting!'" ⅄

Past & Present

Written by: Tor Alexander Valenza Directed by: William F. Gereghty	Guest Cast: Megan Leitch (Ke'ra), Marya Delver (Layale), Jason Gray-Stanford (Orner), Luisa Cianni (Woman)

Faced with a population who appear to be suffering from some form of mass amnesia caused by an apocalyptic event they call the 'Vorlix', SG-1 encounter a bright, beautiful young woman named Ke'ra, who seems to hold some of the clues as to what happened to induce this unenviable state. Whilst she works with Janet Fraiser and Samantha Carter to find a cure for what ails her people, Ke'ra and Daniel find themselves mutually attracted to each other. Sadly, any romance is doomed to failure when investigations reveal Ke'ra to be far more than a simple medic, and is in fact someone SG-1 has met before...

O'Neill

"Oh My! There's a distinct lack of optimism in this room."

"This gives a little insight into Daniel's nicer side," smiles Michael Shanks. "It was an interesting episode certainly from a 'Daniel defending the villain' kind of view. It wasn't typical, so it was important for me to realise that all the things he appeared to be doing out of petulance weren't so much 'whiny' as they were noble. It was very important to me as an actor to be able to motivate those things and not to have Daniel be wrong all the time, and just have someone come in and bale him out."

The actor gives all due credit to Brad Wright who, he insists, "did a very good job of making sure that Daniel was properly motivated, and that the other characters were encouraged into acting in more of a protective way. They were more or less saying to Daniel, 'You may be going through what you're going through, and we'll watch you going through it because we can see and understand your point of view, but at the same time we can't let you be so naïve. We have to watch your back.' I think that led to a very real dynamic between the characters and the situation. I know it certainly helped me play it."

One thing Shanks wasn't so pleased with was the order of play. "It was very odd in the shooting schedule, because that episode came right after 'Forever in a Day' which, though it turned out to be very strange timing, wasn't supposed to be that way. We were actually meant to film 'Past & Present' a few weeks *before* 'Forever in a Day', but the script needed some adjustments, so it kept getting put back. It

Above: A difficult decision has to be made. Hammond and O'Neill in grim mood.

was just the luck of the draw that in the episode immediately after Daniel's wife dies, he decides to make out with another girl! That situation never quite sat right with me, even though I do know that that is just the way television works."

Although it was always the intention to return to the Linea story (after the character was introduced in season two's 'Prisoners'), Jonathan Glassner explains that it wasn't possible to re-visit the original actress: "We decided to go with a different actress for two reasons. First off we couldn't get Bonnie Bartlett, and actually we weren't sure we wanted to. I know she won't mind me saying this, but frankly she was too nice a lady! She wasn't very threatening and we didn't feel that she was a good bad guy. The second reason is that if we had used her, she would have been immediately recognisable, and we wanted to bring Linea back, but surprise the audience when her identity was revealed." ⋏

Jolinar's Memories

Written by: Sonny Wareham and Daniel Stashower	Guest Cast: Carmen Argenziano (Jacob Carter/Selmak), JR Bourne (Martouf), William de Vry (Aldwin), Bob Dawson (Bynarr), Dion Johnstone (Na'onak), Peter Williams (Apophis), David Palffy (Sokar), Tanya Reid (Jolinar)
Directed by: Peter DeLuise	

It's all hellfire and brimstone when the gentle Martouf brings news that Carter's father has been taken prisoner by the System Lord Sokar. Not content to just toss people into dungeons and throw away the key, the Goa'uld has turned a small moon, Netu, into a living Hell, where his unfortunate victims undergo much suffering whilst waiting for their inevitable demise. Determined to rescue Jacob/Selmak's body, or at the very least escape with knowledge vital to the survival of the Tok'ra, Martouf asks Sam to access the memories of his dead wife Jolinar — believed to be the only person ever to have left Netu alive.

'Massive', 'huge' and 'gigantic' are some of the words that spring to mind at the mention of this episode. Jonathan Glassner begins, "It was the largest set I've ever seen. The reason this episode became a two-parter was simply because we couldn't afford to do it as a stand-alone piece. It was almost as expensive as the pilot, 'Children of the Gods'. Robert Cooper, genius that he is, came up with another script which became 'The Devil You Know', and we merged the two budgets together to pay for the whole shebang. It took the crew a couple of months to build the set and we shot it all as one episode."

Amanda Tapping agrees the episodes were big in many ways: "First because I always love episodes with Jacob in them and I always love episodes with Martouf. Then, of course, there was that amazing set. Four storeys of Hell! It was dirty. It was hot. Then there was all the turmoil you could see us going through physically and emotionally." Grinning, she adds, "There was a great atmosphere on that set. It was really *hellish*."

Director Peter DeLuise remembers the efforts taken by director of photography Peter Woeste to get just the right look for the flashback sequences. Whatever the technical term is for such a procedure, Mr

Above: Devlishly clever Sokar.

DeLuise refers to it as "the smeary dreams". Elaborating he says, "'Smeary dreams' is when you shoot at six frames a second, instead of twenty four. What happens is each frame of film is duplicated many times, and, as there is movement, you get a smear. It looks like the residual image of your hand in its first, second, third, fourth position — all in one go. It gives a little bit of a strobing/smearing effect." Offering yet more words of explanation he ventures, "If you've ever been on a drug-induced hallucination then I understand that is what you might encounter!" Perhaps Peter Woeste had been drinking the blood of Sokar. DeLuise is delighted that the hot and heavy atmosphere encountered on Hell was due in no small way to his personal input: "In fact, my contribution to most of the shows that I'm on is to get some big, beefy guys, and show lots of sweat and debauchery because things are just too sterile. We need more dirt!" Å

The Devil You Know

Written by: Robert C. Cooper
Directed by: Peter DeLuise

Guest Cast: Carmen Argenziano (Jacob Carter/ Selmak), JR Bourne (Martouf), William de Vry (Aldwin), Bob Dawson (Bynarr), Peter Williams (Apophis), Dion Johnstone (Na'onak), David Palffy (Sokar), Tanya Reid (Jolinar)

The attempt to rescue Jacob Carter ends with O'Neill, Sam Carter, Daniel and Martouf being captured by their old nemesis, Apophis. Using a hallucinogenic drug appropriately named 'the blood of Sokar', he tries to coax information from their befuddled minds that he believes is crucial to his bid to overthrow Sokar. Aware that the original rescue attempt has failed, the Tok'ra deliver a bomb they insist must be used to destroy the moon, its inhabitants and all nearby ships. Teal'c must rely on his expert monitoring of the situation and knowledge of Apophis's *modus operandi* to pluck his friends to safety.

O'Neill

"They gave me something that reminded me of the 70s."

Writer Robert Cooper confirms that this episode really came about because of economics: "A team of writers had pitched the story that eventually became part one, the essence being SG-1 is recruited to save Jacob, who has been captured by a Goa'uld whilst working undercover. We liked the idea because it involved a rescue mission to save Jacob, a character that Sam obviously has a close emotional connection to, but also because it explored the consequences of Jacob becoming a Tok'ra host to save himself from cancer. We developed the story more and hooked into the concept that the place where he had been sent would be the Goa'uld version of Hell. When the script finally came in, we realised that we couldn't afford to build the set that was the centrepiece for the episode. So, we quickly scrambled and tried to come up with a story for another

Sokar

Sokar is the one of the most powerful of all the Goa'uld System Lords. To the people of Earth, he is the very embodiment of evil, and is known by a slightly different name: Satan. Banished by the other Lords because of his wild and wicked ways, Sokar returned to his home world of Delmak and proceeded to give everybody Hell.

episode that could take place in that set — thus amortising the cost over two episodes — and 'The Devil You Know' was born. In the end all the scrambling was worth it, not least because the set was so magnificent it won a well-deserved Gemini for our talented production design team!"

Robert Cooper continues by revealing, "Some people have wondered why we created this really cool Goa'uld in Sokar, only to kill him off right away. Well, we originally killed Apophis because the character had gotten a little weak. We had beaten him so many times that he was no longer scary. Then we realised we could bring him back in dramatic fashion, and give his character a whole new level by having him rise from the ashes and take over the realm of the scariest Goa'uld we could think of. We built Sokar up exactly for this reason. The more powerful he was, the more powerful Apophis would become when he defeated him."

Having commented on the great manicure sported by Sokar, Peter DeLuise goes on, "The nails were inspired by the character played by Robert DeNiro in *Angel Heart*. Sokar's eyes were an homage to Darth Maul in *The Phantom Menace*, and the albino look and the hood were from the classic evil Emperor, that Ian McDairmid played in *Return of the Jedi*. You know, when Sokar is just sitting there, wallowing in his own filth, I reminded [actor] David Palffy of Bela Lugosi, of his grace and stillness, and he played that to great effect." ⋏

Foothold

Written by: Heather E. Ash
Directed by: Andy Mikita

Guest Cast: Tom McBeath (Colonel Harry Maybourne), Colin Cunningham (Major Davis), Richard Leacock (Colonel Brogen), Colin Lawrence (Sergeant Warren), Dan Shea (Sergeant Siler)

D odgy dealings are afoot when a group of aliens manage to infiltrate the SGC by taking on the looks and personality of the personnel. Oblivious to the danger, the SG-1 team is knocked unconscious by an unhealthy dose of sedative jabbed into their nether regions by a bogus Janet Fraiser and her nursing staff. Teal'c is the first member of SG-1 to awake and realise the perilous situation. He manages to hold the hostile visitors at bay whilst Sam Carter escapes Cheyenne Mountain and informs Colonel Maybourne of the 'Foothold' crisis. Completely taken in by two creatures purporting to be O'Neill and Daniel Jackson, Maybourne persuades Carter to return with him and the others only to discover that appearances can be more than deceptive.

Carter

"Maybourne, you are an idiot every day of the week. Why couldn't you have taken one day off?"

A difficult episode by anyone's standards, writer Heather Ash admits, "This was an extremely hard script to write, even to conceptualise. We spent a lot of time trying to figure it out — who and what the aliens were, what they wanted, if our characters were aware of them. Once we'd settled on the 'invasion' model, and the need to get Carter off the base, we had to figure out whom she'd go to for help. Originally, she sought Major Davis's help. Later, we decided it would be more compelling to have her join with Colonel Maybourne, the one person she couldn't trust."

Whilst he may seem a very slimy piece of work in the series, Colonel Maybourne's alter ego, actor Tom McBeath, couldn't be further from that image. "When we cast Tom," begins Jonathan Glassner in executive producer mode, "it was very similar to when we cast Robert Duncan in 'Seth', in that most of the people that came in were these big, mean-looking guys. Tom is kind of this scrawny, little guy who, when you get to meet him, is the sweetest, most gentle person you could wish to know. Having him act against type like that and letting him have fun with it actually worked out very well."

Above: The arrival of some unwelcome visitors.

Amanda Tapping concurs, "Tom McBeath is an amazing actor and a really wonderful guy, so it's very hard to hate him. It's always a big acting challenge when you have to hate someone so sweet." Tapping was extremely taken with the episode for many reasons, not least because it gave her "the chance to be able to show that dichotomy of not trusting. Carter — who follows military rules and does everything the way she's supposed to — suddenly turns her back on everything saying, 'Nah! I don't trust you guys.'" The actress has particularly fond memories of the scene in the café: "I came up with that line — the 'Maybourne, you're an idiot every day of the week. Why couldn't you have taken one day off?' line." Thrilled she yells, "That was me! I was looking at one of the fan websites which talks about favourite SG-1 lines and there it was, right up there." Doing a fair impression of Homer Simpson she whoops, "When I saw that, it was like one of those 'Woohoo' moments."

There were noises of a less joyous kind from the poor cast members who had literally been strung up for most of the day. "It was the only time I ever heard Don Davis complain," laughs Ash, "and even then he only said, 'Sometimes I wonder what goes on in that writer's brain of yours.'" ⋏

Pretense

Written by: Kathryn Powers Directed by: David Warry-Smith	Guest Cast: Alexis Cruz (Skaara/Klorel), Frida Betrani (Lya), Marie Stillin (Travell), Garwin Sanford (Narim), Kevin Durand (Zipacna)

Two members of SG-1 take part in a custody battle with a difference when the Tollan, Narim, appears at the SGC with an invitation for them to take part in an ancient ceremony which will determine which personality has control over the body of Daniel's brother-in-law, Skaara. Taken as host by Klorel (Apophis's adopted son), the Goa'uld claims his is the dominant force and should be allowed to survive at whatever cost to the body and mind of the human. Whilst Daniel and O'Neill plead Skaara's case, it becomes clear to Sam and Teal'c that the Goa'uld chosen to speak for Klorel has an ulterior motive for being on the Tollan home world.

O'Neill

"The Tollan will guarantee your safety? Is that a 'money back if you're not completely alive' guarantee?"

Honest to a fault, the first thing executive producer Brad Wright has to say about 'Pretense' is, "I didn't really like it. It was a Kathryn Powers script that Jonathan re-wrote fairly heavily." Glassner himself admits that he often gets confused when credited with writing the story, "Because, even though I did write half of it, I tend to think of it as Kathryn's." Wright goes on, "Jonathan was always more keen on the story than I was, but that was because he was leaving at the end of season three, and there were a couple of things he wanted to wrap up, including the Skaara/Klorel arc." Wright agrees that the decision of the show's co-creator made perfect sense: "It meant we could create new threats and new characters, but I'm not that crazy about the episode because I never did like the device that allowed Skaara to talk freely. Also, I didn't like how Skaara just disappeared and went happily back to Abydos after

Ion Cannon

The Tollan's first line of defence. The Ion Cannon is a weapon so powerful, it is capable of destroying a Goa'uld mothership with one shot. The Tollan's reluctance to share technology with the humans means this highly effective war toy remains outside the US military's arsenal.

Above: Carter and Teal'c keep an eye on developments.

the Triad. It struck me that there would be far too much baggage." Wright feels that 'Pretense' was a very interesting psychological story: "It was almost the Picard story from *The Next Generation* where he returns after having been a Borg. Skaara had been a Goa'uld. He's killed millions but — well — he just goes happily home." In defence, Jonathan Glassner offers, "Since Alexis Cruz was a semi-regular on another series, it was more difficult to bring him back and conclude that story line, so we had to go with what we could get."

Wright may not have been totally thrilled with the overall result, but does feel the episode had some redeeming factors: "It was a way of going back and meeting the Tollan again. It was always difficult to come up with stories that involved the Tollan, but I always liked them as a kind of bureaucratic balance. Through them we got to glimpse the kind of future that we on Earth would probably not want to become involved with. They were the kinds of humans I hope we *don't* evolve into being."

Agreeing that the po-faced individuals are too uptight for their own good, Wright says, "They don't have a lot of whimsy. Their lives are all about order and rules and of course, that all comes tumbling down around them in a later episode... But I guess, even if it isn't close to my favourite story, I liked the fact that it was another insightful window into the Tollan personality." ᚨ

Urgo

Written by: Tor Alexander Valenza

Directed by: Peter DeLuise

Guest cast: Dom DeLuise (Urgo/Togar), Nickolas Baric (SF Guard), Bill Nikolai (Technician)

Madness and mayhem disrupts the smooth running of the SGC when the top team returns from a seemingly routine mission with a fifth, unseen member. Insatiably curious and terminally bored, the fun-loving Urgo has implanted himself into the minds of SG-1, apparently to investigate and record new experiences. In exchange he provides them with the ability to function as one, and heightens their sensory perceptions. Unfortunately, SG-1's interaction with their invisible friend results in the group being relieved of duty and confined to barracks until a way can be found to remove the impish Urgo from their brains.

Hammond to O'Neill

"Can we determine what threat they pose to the base?"

"Apparently all desserts on base are in grave danger."

Without a doubt, 'Urgo' is a favourite amongst favourites. "There aren't enough good things we could say about working with Dom DeLuise on that episode," states Amanda Tapping. "We were all in hysterics the whole time. Peter would start the cameras rolling and then yell, 'Hey, Dad! Just make up stuff at the end of the scene and make them laugh and… Action!' We didn't stand a chance."

A fun experience on and off screen, Brad Wright says that 'Urgo' is the one that will stick in his mind forever. "Dom DeLuise had been a huge fan of *Stargate* since the beginning, and because we love his work so much we invited him to be in our show. Of course, we all decided that if Dom took up the invitation then an episode would have to be written especially for him. Not that he took much notice of the lines! He'd just do his own thing, but it was hilarious. I've never known the cast or crew laugh so much."

Richard Dean Anderson, an occasional stranger to the script himself, remembers, "The most difficult thing about getting through each scene was getting Dom to settle down, and I mean that in the nicest way," he grins. "The most fun we had happened off camera, of course, but editing what was *on* camera became the biggest challenge because Dom is the most improvisational and spontaneous actor. It was great fun just to watch him fly off in all kinds of directions. The absolute joy of

44 STARGATE THE ILLUSTRATED COMPANION

working on that episode was watching the father/son dynamic, with Peter trying to rein in his Dad enough to get the stuff that we needed to tell the story." Anderson's only regret is, "We didn't have enough time to show all of the wonderful comedy that DeLuise is a genius at."

Peter DeLuise claims he simply couldn't rein his father in. "What I did do," he says, "was remind the writers, who take great pains to make all the words make sense, that my father has a 'loosey goosey' approach to improvisation, and doesn't always stick to the written word. But the whole trick to making that work was that my Dad's character was a free spirit, and therefore had lots of licence. He could be the cross charac- terisation of all four main characters. He could be the id — the pleasure centre of all four brains, so he had great licence to do what he wanted. So I just kept a camera on him, and you can see how I staged most of the scenes he's in — he's tormenting people!" Director DeLuise is for- ever grateful to Brad Wright for turning what transpired to be the most film ever shot on the show into something short enough for television. "Brad picked out the best bits, but the foul-mouthed 'European version' is around somewhere!" ⅄

Above: Confronted by Urgo's awesome good looks, Teal'c struggles to keep a stony face.

A Hundred Days

Story by: Victoria C. James	Guest Cast: Michele Green (Laira), Julie Patzwald
Teleplay by: Brad Wright	(Naytha), Gary Jones (Technician), Shane Meier
Directed by: David	(Garan), Marcel Maillard (Paynan)
Warry-Smith	

When SG-1 have a starlit encounter with the magical 'fire rain' of Edora they realise that far from being the recipients of a spectacular show of falling stars, the inhabitants of a small village are in grave danger from falling debris from an asteroid belt. Breaking away from the main group to rescue the village leader's son, Jack O'Neill is left stranded on the planet when a meteor strikes the Stargate site, burying it under tons of rubble. Earthside, Sam Carter works around the clock trying to find a way to retrieve their lost colleague. With hope of his returning home diminishing with each day, O'Neill and the village leader, Laira, develop their growing romantic attachment into something both believe will become more permanent.

> **O'Neill**
>
> "Teal'c! You are one stubborn son of a bitch!"

Ever realised that Brad Wright was a playwright before he made the transfer to television? "He used to write plays, and that's what gave him the writing bug and set him on his way," reports Jonathan Glassner. "One of the things Brad is really good at is writing episodes that are very dramatic, and don't need that much 'gung ho' action in them. You could produce many of Brad's episodes on a theatre stage. He wrote a lot for *The Outer Limits* like that, and *Stargate*'s season one story 'Solitudes' — the one set on the ice crevasse — was another great example of Brad's skill."

Wright is very modest about his achievement. "'A Hundred Days' began as an idea our script coordinator, Victoria James, came up with

Fire Rain

A spectacular phenomenon watched by the inhabitants of Edora on the same night every year, the Fire Rain is actually a meteor shower caused when the planet's orbit passes through an asteroid belt. As deadly as it is beautiful, the irregularity of Edora's orbit means that some Fire Rain actually strikes the ground every 150 years, causing catastrophic damage and loss of life.

about a planet which was bombarded by comets every few hundred years. I ran with that, and it became a love story. It's one of those 'love it or hate it' episodes for most fans, and my own feeling falls somewhere in between. At the last Gatecon in Vancouver, several fans told me that O'Neill would *never* give up on going home, and that I was wrong to suggest he would go native after only three months." Wright suggests the episode might have been a good two-parter, and that there could be more of the story to tell. Watch this space…

Above: Laira and O'Neill — up close and personal.

From a fan's point of view, one of the mysteries remaining at the end of the episode was the question of whether or not O'Neill had been successful in helping Laira achieve her wish for a child. Asked if he thought the Colonel would have walked off and returned to Earth under those circumstances Richard Dean Anderson replies, "Well, if he knew — no! Of course he wouldn't have. For the story's sake and for the 'potential for intrigue' sake he was able to walk away — albeit somewhat sadly. But in real life I don't think he would have walked away at all." Smiling, he goes on, "As for what we might do with the story, now that everyone except O'Neill knows he might have impregnated a woman and have a child somewhere in another part of the galaxy — who knows? Stay tuned." ㅅ

Shades of Grey

Written by: Jonathan Glassner
Directed by: Martin Wood

Guest Cast: Tom McBeath (Colonel Harry Maybourne), Steve Makaj (Colonel Makepeace), Marie Stilling (Travell), Christian Bocher (Major Newman), Linnea Sharples (Lieutenant Clare Tobias)

Jack O'Neill astounds his comrades and appears to show his true colours when he steals a weapon-disarming device during a diplomatic mission to Tollana. Unrepentant, he is forced to accept early retirement and deliberately turns his back on even his closest friends at the SGC. Secretly joining forces with the ubiquitous Colonel Maybourne and his cronies, O'Neill decides to 'take' whatever he feels is necessary rather than promote mutual trade or diplomacy. His last official request is that he be allowed to return to Edora to continue his relationship with the woman he left behind, but this trip through the Stargate hides a much darker purpose.

O'Neill

"I'd rather be a thief and alive than honest and dead."

Jonathan Glassner credits Richard Dean Anderson with the idea for this episode: "Rick came in one day and said he wanted to shake up the character of O'Neill somehow, and wanted to explore his dark side. He actually wanted O'Neill to go *really* bad, but Brad and I had a think about it and realised that was probably going too far — that it might be irredeemable if our hero went completely off the rails. However, it did give me the idea of having the character *fake* that he'd gone bad, in order to flush out some really nasty characters."

Speaking of nasties, director Martin Wood shares the majority opinion that Colonel Maybourne is one of the worst. "Now, that character is *greasy*," he nods. "You know, in some of the later episodes he kind of ends up helping SG-1 but always, when you come away from him — when you pull away from a handshake with him — you want to wipe your hand. And even if he was giving you flowers, you'd find there were wasps in there, or some weird poison he was testing that you'd carry with you. We've had some greasy characters but he is definitely one of the worst — or best, depending on how you look at it." The director did manage to inveigle some payback for Maybourne's misdeeds. "When he comes back in season four's 'Chain Reaction', I make him eat hotdog after hotdog after hotdog for being so nasty to SG-1!"

Away from oily gents, Wood had some oiling of wheels to do to get a particular idea in motion: "One of the devices we wanted to create to make the story work was a revolving Stargate. There's a really cool shot where O'Neill walks through one gate and right out of the other, and the idea I had (which everybody hates still) was that we follow O'Neill from the Earth Gateroom and go right through with him to the off world Gateroom (which was ours, covered in plastic), but look at it from *outside* the Stargate. We did it by panning along with him going past the Stargate, so essentially we split the Stargate in half. I felt that is what it should look like: there wouldn't be a time lag — O'Neill would just walk in one side and out through the other. It's what SG-1 do all the time." Wood claims that when he suggested this in the production meeting he was shouted down with cries of, "Oh that can't happen!" "You know sometimes the guys have a tendency to over-think these things but, unusually, Michael Greenburg was my strongest supporter. He's the one who actually said 'We're doing it,' so we did." Λ

Above: O'Neill and Newman keep their eyes on the ball.

New Ground

Written by: Heather E. Ash	Guest Cast: Richard Ian Cox (Nyan), Daryl Shuttleworth
Directed by: Chris McMullin	(Commander Rigar), Desiree Zuroski (Parcy), Jennifer
	Copping (Malin)

S G-1 faces an uncomfortable time when they are unwittingly caught up in a war between the Opticans and the Bedrosians, two cultures diametrically opposed in their evolutionary beliefs. Daniel, Carter and O'Neill are held captive in tiny cages and subjected to humiliating torture by the leader of some hardline soldiers, whilst Teal'c receives altogether more humanitarian treatment at the hands of a young Bedrosian scientist. The Jaffa was badly injured and blinded during an escape attempt but is helped to safety by the young man. Teal'c must trust both Nyan's medical skill and willingness to learn if he is to facilitate SG-1's route off the planet.

O'Neill

"Hey Rigar! You know that 'we come in peace' business? Bite me!"

"I conceived this episode thinking of evolution," says writer Heather Ash. "What if we went to a planet, a former Goa'uld colony, that believed in evolution… and they were wrong?" Acknowledging the executive producers of the show Ash goes on, "Brad Wright and Robert Cooper really helped get the action into the episode. Plus it was a great opportunity to see Teal'c in a new position, an utterly helpless warrior dependent on someone he didn't trust. Christopher Judge did a fantastic job."

Christopher Judge welcomed the opportunity to portray a rarely seen side of Teal'c: "So much of my character is based on the fact that anything that afflicts me is quickly healed by my symbiote, but here we tried something that was going to take a while. Many actors will play blind as helpless. I chose to show Teal'c dealing with the fact that all his other senses were sharpened. It was quite the challenge for me to act as though objects were flying all around me, because I don't think that flapping my arms at things that aren't there is one of the skills at which I excel!"

Appropriately, some might tease, the two opposing sides in the episode were named after Ash's agent and an executive from the television company. "My agent, Matt Bedrosian, gave his name to one side," she admits, "whilst the Opticans were a variation of Tony Optican, who used to work for MGM."

The episode has less than positive memories for Jonathan Glassner.

Above: The Bedrosians have ways of making O'Neill talk.

"We had more than our share of production problems because of where we were shooting," he sighs. "We had a Stargate that was buried in the wall of a cliff face, which was really difficult to do, because the blue screen that needs to be there for the Kawoosh needs to be a good way behind the Stargate. It can't be immediately behind the circle because the effect wouldn't be right. But what you see is a real cliff, so what we had to do was build an extension out far enough to be able to get the screen far enough behind it. That gave us a lot of headaches, but the perseverance paid off and it ended up working out just fine."

Whilst Ash can't remember any specific complaints during filming, Glassner points out, "The actors were kind of upset at having to sit in those cages forever!" Ash adds, "More bothersome was the large amount of dust in the air from the dirt shipped in to cover the floors of the tent." Needless to say Amanda Tapping didn't mind this at all. A tom-boy to the last she smirks, "The ones where I get totally, disgustingly filthy are the best!" Ash especially liked the realistic conclusion to the episode. "I loved that, at the end, we don't stick around and try to convince people of reality. We just get the hell outta Dodge." ⋏

Maternal Instinct

Written by: Robert C. Cooper **Directed by:** Peter Woeste	**Guest Cast:** Tony Amendola (Bra'tac), Terry Chen (Monk), Aaron Douglas (Moac), Steve Bacic (Major Coburn), Carla Boudrea (Oma Desala)

SG-1 become involved in a race against time to find a lost world and retrieve the child hidden by Daniel's wife, before Apophis discovers and absconds with the boy. Custodian of the combined knowledge of the Goa'uld, the child's wisdom could enable Apophis to rule over all the other System Lords. Using Daniel's knowledge of the past and Bra'tac's confirmation of traditional fables, they scour the Stargate addresses in the computer database till they come up with the planet most likely to be the legendary Kheb. Once there, Daniel's willingness to walk the path to Enlightenment enables the rest to see that there is more than one way to overcome the Goa'uld's military might.

The Monk

"Learn the path through the darkness into the next life."

"This is the first of what I like to call the 'Glowing Alien Arc'," offers writer Robert Cooper. "When Sha're died in 'Forever in a Day', Daniel Jackson's purpose for being a part of the Stargate programme became a little cloudy. So, we invented a quest that could be bestowed on Daniel by Sha're before she died, and that was to find and protect the Harsesis child. To be honest I just wanted to write a real 'Daniel episode' where he would get to use his linguist/social skills and I could have some fun with Zen Kohns. The banter between O'Neill and Daniel in this one really set a new level that we all tried to play on in future scenes between the two."

Michael Shanks certainly enjoyed the episode, although admits to being less of a spiritual being than Daniel Jackson: "The character is a lot more in that vein than I. It's funny because when I was trying to understand this more spiritual point of view, I couldn't quite get into the mindset. I wasn't as comfortable with the whole Buddhist journey as probably a lot of other actors on our show would be. I'm a bit more closed minded!" Ironically, the actor says he gets lots of poetry and books in the mail because "fans think I'm like Daniel and am a wonderful, sensitive guy. But my girlfriend says, 'Yeah! But they don't know you.' I have to admit that I am a little bit more cynical about that type of path and though that's not necessarily for the better, that's just me."

Above: O'Neill surveys the Path to Enlightenment.

One thing Shanks found remarkably easy was his relationship with the twin boys who played the Harsesis child: "That was a lovely experience. My daughter was just over a year old when we made the episode, so I was used to handling babies. We had a very limited time on set with the boys and one was always upset, so that was the one we tried to film with first, but I just got comfortable with them and we managed to capture a couple of magic moments of interaction with them. The first one is when Daniel first sees the baby in the chamber. I came up and just as the camera moved off me and on to the baby I stayed right by him and made some sort of 'googoo gaga' face to him. The baby was looking up at me and his reaction was just so warm. It was like 'Hey! Buddy!', and suited the situation perfectly. The second was when I was about to hand the baby back to Oma Desala and he clung on to my shirt. Those are moments which would be very difficult to reproduce, but were wonderful to experience and capture on film." ⋏

Crystal Skull

Story by: Michael Greenburg and Jarrad Paul
Teleplay by: Brad Wright
Directed by: Brad Turner

Guest cast: Jan Rubes (Nicholas Ballard), Jason Schombing (Robert Rothman), Dan Shea (Sergeant Siler), Russell Roberts (Psychiatrist), Jacquie Janzen (Nurse), Christopher Judge (Voice of Quetlzelcoatl)

P oor Daniel Jackson is neither seen nor heard when the emissions given off by a crystal skull cause a phase shift rendering him invisible to those on Earth. Unable to determine what's happened to the archaeologist, the scientists at the SGC try unsuccessfully to unravel the mystery of the ancient artefact. In desperation, SG-1 turn to Daniel's grandfather, Nicholas Ballard, once a scientist of some note, now a voluntary patient in an asylum. An earlier experience with the skull has left Nick with the ability to see and hear Daniel, and together they work out that the answer to the problem is for Daniel to revisit the chamber where the skull was found and ask the 'giants' there for help.

Rothman to Siler

"Teleportation Device? What do you think?"

"I think you're going to get fired."

Innovative in every sense from storyline to visual effects, this episode really brought out the team ethic of the *Stargate* gang. Based on an idea broached by executive producer Michael Greenburg and his godson Jarrad Paul, Michael Shanks is thrilled to have been given the opportunity to input some writing ideas. "I had been in the process of trying to write a *Stargate* script based on a piece of mythology about a crystal skull," he recalls. The idea had been planted when the actor was given a book full of the mysteries of South America by one of the generator operators at the Bridge Studios in Vancouver. "This book was so incred-

Crystal Skulls

It's one of Earth's most intriguing real-life mysteries: who made the ancient crystal skulls that have been found by archaeologists in burial sites throughout Mexico and South America, and what is their purpose? They seem to have been made using techniques far in advance of their time, which had led many to suggest they were crafted by an alien race. Others believe that if thirteen of the oldest skulls are brought together in one place, mystical forces will be unleashed...

ible," expounds Shanks, "because what it does is point out the inconsistencies of modern archaeological known facts with actual unexplained
discoveries and phenomena. Apparently these finds are not reported in
mainstream venues because they go against contemporary archaeological beliefs and would, therefore, rock the boat and ask questions that we
can't answer at this time."

Above: Daniel and Nick investigate the source of their problems.

Grateful to Michael Greenburg for giving him such a wonderful
opportunity, Shanks says, "I thought the myth about the crystal skulls
would make a great story for *Stargate* and started to write it. At the same
time, Michael and Paul came up with this other idea that they pitched
where Rick's character goes on this journey of discovery. But Rick said,
'Nah! I did that in *MacGyver*. I don't want to do it again.' So Michael
turned to me and said, 'Take this outline and see if you can add to it.' I
did, then Brad Wright took all of this mish mash and put it together,
resulting in 'Crystal Skull'. I don't think the end result was exactly as
Michael or I had envisaged, but most of the concepts remained and my
strongest ideas, those of Daniel's grandfather and the idea of the crystal
skull, were retained. To me it was a great episode because I got to see it
from a writer's point of view and it is really something to watch a figment
of your imagination come to life on screen." λ

Nemesis

Written by: Robert C. Cooper	Guest Cast: Colin Cunningham (Major Davis), Gary
Directed by: Martin Wood	Jones (Technician), Guyle Lee-Fraiser (Technician #2)

With Daniel laid low in the infirmary, the rest of SG-1 look forward to a week of much needed R & R, but instead find themselves plunged into the most crucial battle for survival yet. Beamed aboard Thor's ship, O'Neill learns that the 'nasty technobugs' invading the Asgard vessel are in fact an even bigger threat to the universe than the Goa'uld. Thor insists the only way to stop the invasion is to destroy the ship before it reaches Earth's atmosphere. Prepared to die for the future of Mankind, O'Neill orders a massive amount of explosives to be transported on to the ship, and is less than thrilled when Carter and Teal'c arrive with them. Embarking on a series of individually heroic actions, the three team members use every skill they possess to try to save the day.

O'Neill to Teal'c

"Say something."

"One small step for Jaffa."

"Very nice."

"Almost every year I've directed the end of season episode and this was the first one that scared me," admits Martin Wood. "It was like, 'Oh man!' because suddenly there's these new critters — the Replicators — so a lot of research and development had to be done to get them right." Affirming that he and visual effects producer James Tichenor share a desire to make any effect 'organic' ie part of everyday life, the director explains, "It's like when the Stargate opens... I don't cut to it every time it goes Kawoosh because we've seen it a million times, and the characters don't react to it in the same way anymore. They see it every day, so it's no big deal." Wood wanted to create the same feeling with the new technobugs. "The Replicators are creatures that are all over the place. They are ubiquitous and I wanted to make it look as though they were

Replicators

Artificial intelligences resembling spiders. Originally brought to the Asgard home world by accident, they feed off metals and alloys and quickly produce copies of themselves. Able to replicate in plague proportions they have quickly become the biggest threat the Asgard and humans have ever faced.

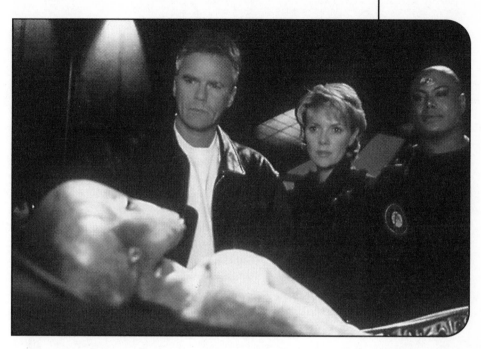

Above: Genuine concern for an ailing friend.

literally coming from anywhere, anytime. The first time we see them is when O'Neill is walking through the halls of Thor's ship, and as well as hearing and seeing them, one actually had to touch him. When Rick asked 'Why?' I told him that we had to know that they weren't going to kill him straight off."

The director explains that this view was borne out of some of his experiences during an expedition to Africa: "We're so used to animals running away from us here, but in Africa, I found that they walked towards you because they don't care, and don't know what you are. You could be lunch!" Wood transferred this attitude to the Replicators, "These creatures don't know what human beings are, so they are going to scuttle over to O'Neill. They don't know whether to be scared or to be angry. He's not mechanical. He's not what they are looking for, so they just feel him out and walk past. He's no threat."

Whilst the rest of us may be a little scared of the beasties, Wood isn't. "The Replicators aren't particularly effective bad guys for me because they don't have faces, they don't have personalities, and you can hear them coming! I'm more scared of spiders, because you can look up at the ceiling and see a beam or a post and silently this thing crawls from behind it. I only think things are scary if you can't hear them coming." Λ

Small Victories

Written by: Robert C. Cooper	Guest cast: Colin Cunningham (Major Davis), Gary
Directed by: Martin Wood	Jones (Technician), Dan Shea (Sergeant Siler), Yurij Kis
	(Yuri), Dmitry Chepovetsky (Boris)

The SG-1 makes a triumphant return to base thinking that the Earth has been saved from the Replicators. Sadly, one of the creatures survived when Thor's ship crashed into the sea, and has boarded a Russian submarine, killing the entire crew. As the creature continues to replicate at an alarming rate, it seems to O'Neill that the best option is to tow the sub out to open waters and blast it with a nuclear missile. Overruled by cautious government types determined to avoid a conflict with the Russians, it's left to the Colonel, Teal'c and a small elite force to try to overcome the bugs by close combat. Meanwhile, Carter is transported to the Asgard home planet, as the aliens believe she may be able to come up with a plan to defeat their destructive enemy.

O'Neill

"I'd be happy to debrief you all, after I've debriefed myself for a nice hot shower."

Director Martin Wood says there are two things that will forever stick in his memory from the filming of this episode, aside from the fact that producer John Smith's budget gave him a lot of leeway to be able to shoot it like a mini-movie. Firstly, the location: filming took place in a real Russian submarine, Foxtrot class, called *The Blackbird*. "This thing was very small, very cramped and very malevolent," Wood laughs. "Russian engineers must have walked through the sub making sure that every possible danger was incorporated into its design. It was like — 'You can run here, so make sure there is a sharp point to catch on.'"

Ever in search of the perfect shot, Wood had one unfortunate individual climb inside the torpedo tube, just to tip water from a bucket out onto the actors each time they opened the tube door! "Scott from visual effects deserves so much credit because I hadn't even thought about how scary that might be, until I had to get in and shoot something myself. The tube was like a steel coffin. I'm quite broad shouldered, so I was touching the sides of the thing. I was squeezed in tight, and then when Jim Menard the DP [director of photography] shut the door it went completely dark, completely silent, there was no air movement and they couldn't hear me. I was screaming for them to open the door but they couldn't hear a sound.

Above: Machiavellian
Meccano — a deadly
Replicator.

Eventually Jim opens the door and I'm hanging out, hyperventilating — a wreck. Jim says to me, 'Are you claustrophobic?' and I gasped, 'I am now!' I looked at Scott and thought he was one of the bravest guys around. I was only in there for a few seconds, but he was in there for ten minutes. I'm proud to be able to say we belong to a very elite club of people who've been inside the torpedo tube of a Russian submarine."

Not content with being terrified inside the barrel of a gun, Wood also had a scary moment as a result of fire from a gun: "There's a shot when we see things from Teal'c's point of view as he blasts the Replicators that have just killed his partner. Well, the automatic shot guns we were using have this five-foot flame that comes out when they're fired. Our camera operator takes a look at this and says, 'Er, OK, I've had enough!' so I ended up taking the shot. The concussion from these guns is so strong it actually knocks the camera back, and the noise in a confined space is deafening. But it was great! I mean, normal people just don't get to do these kinds of things." We should be grateful for small mercies... Λ

The Other Side

Written by: Brad Wright	Guest Cast: Rene Auberjonois (Alar), Anne Marie
Directed by: Peter DeLuise	Loder (Farrell), Gary Jones (Technician Sergeant
	Davis), Dan Shea (Sergeant Siler), Stephen Park
	(Controller), Kyle Cassie (Eurondan soldier), Kris
	Keeler (Zombie Pilot Ollan)

The answer to SGC's and Earth's prayer seems to have come in the form of the Eurondans, a people who claim to be under attack and in need of assistance. In return for what he sees as immediate humanitarian aid, the leader of the Eurondan people offers the information to build advanced technology that could help Earth's fight against the Goa'uld. All he asks in exchange is unlimited amounts of heavy water — the waste product from nuclear fission — a deal to which O'Neill quickly agrees. Trusting his instincts and knowledge of cultures ancient and modern, Daniel Jackson is the only member of SG-1 who voices the opinion that the Eurondans might not be as trustworthy as they seem, until a chance comment sets O'Neill thinking that their new friends may hold beliefs of a more sinister nature.

Teal'c to O'Neill

"He is concealing something."

"Like what?"

"I am unsure. He is concealing it."

"What I really wanted to do with this episode," explains writer Brad Wright, "is explore what happened if the people that we befriend, who give us everything that we really, really want, end up being bad guys not worthy of our friendship. It's something I explored with the Aschen too [in '2010']. I love the 'be careful who you get into bed with. Be careful what you wish for' theme. I also wanted to explain the philosophical question, 'Why don't our allies throw technology our way?' There is a rationale, and part of it lies in the fact that anyone who is willing to just give stuff probably isn't truly aware of its power from an ethical perspective." Objective about his work, Wright says if he had to do it all again, he would have been a little less heavy handed, but concedes, "I wanted to peel the onion a little more slowly, but in forty minutes you can't really do justice to such a deep concept."

Wright loved the dynamic between O'Neill and Daniel in that episode but admits to getting a serious amount of criticism from fans: "They thought I was trying to put a wedge between the characters, but

Above: Alar holds the key to a world's destruction.

all I was trying to do was embrace what I perceived as a nice capability between the two actors. My favourite piece of dialogue is where they go, 'Jack?', 'Daniel?', 'What are you doing?' and it goes back and forth between them. And I really liked that O'Neill was dead wrong and admitted it."

Although he agrees that Alar (a memorable performance by *Star Trek: Deep Space Nine*'s Rene Auberjonois) "had it coming", the writer is bothered by one choice Richard Dean Anderson made, which Wright feels made quite a difference to how the ending was viewed. "After he had deliberately closed the iris, knowing he was committing Alar to death, he was supposed to have said, 'This is where we came in.' In other words, O'Neill's justification was the Eurondans were moribund. They were an inch away from their own doom and then we came in and bought them some time. My feeling is that the line would have helped to make the episode more symmetrical but, you know, writers are like that and actors aren't." ⋏

Upgrades

Written by: David Rich	Guest cast: Vanessa Angel (Anise/Freya), Dan Shea
Directed by: Martin Wood	(Sergeant Siler), Kristina Copeland (Waitress), Frank Topol (Big Guy), Fraser Attcheson (Jaffa Commander)

There's more than a hint of, 'Is it a bird? Is it a plane? No, it's SG-1!' when Anise, a new Tok'ra representative to Earth, comes bearing gifts. Invited to test some mysterious devices the Tok'ra believe could prove valuable in the fight against the Goa'uld, the human members of SG-1 find themselves equipped with super-human physical abilities. Delighted to find themselves faster than speeding bullets, their enthusiasm for the new armbands wavers only slightly when they find they can't take them off. Even though Dr Fraiser's medical evidence shows they could be in grave danger from the devices, SG-1 decides to ignore standing orders and dash off to inflict as much damage as possible on Apophis's latest building project, before their energy — or snacks — run out.

> ## Hammond
>
> "I thought the devices were supposed to enhance them physically, not make them stupid."

Brad Wright confides that this episode started with an idea from writer David Rich, suggesting armbands that gave SG-1 super powers: "It was a great concept and David and I spun it from there. However, David's eventual script was so ambitious that it unfortunately came under the heading of 'unproduceable'. We just wouldn't have been able to make the script that he wrote, so Robert Cooper jumped in and did a deft, quick and I think fairly expert rewrite of the episode, embracing the humour angle. I said, 'Look! If we're going to do Superman, we have to play it, to a certain extent, for the humour.'"

Wright is delighted that Cooper managed to incorporate one of Wright's dearest wishes into the show. "I loved the fight in the bar," he grins. "That entire scene came about because of my complete, unabashed desire for a bar fight. Robert asked why I wanted one, to which I replied, 'Because it would be so cool!' He went through hoops to try to make that scene work, God bless him — and it did."

Director Martin Wood points out that someone else was also going through hoops: Kenny Gibbs, who was in charge of the props on set. "The thing that killed me was those armbands — they never worked! They were these mechanical devices that cost thousands of dollars, and

every day Dave Sinclair, the property master, would hand one of these to Kenny, and Kenny would snap it on the actor, and it wouldn't stay. They were supposed to open and close on their own but they wouldn't. Kenny and Dave would work all night on them, and every day filming would be held up because these armbands wouldn't work. So I started calling Kenny 'Evil Kenny' and it's just stuck. He's called that to this day!"

Not all the effects cost thousands of dollars, and some of them even worked. The 'device' used to represent the force shield was a stroke of genius from director of photography Jim Menard. Martin Wood describes how he and visual effects supervisor James Tichenor were ruminating on how to achieve the complicated effect when Menard jokingly suggested they use a big sheet of cling film. "I thought it was a great idea," laughs Wood. "So we went out to the craft service table, got some cling film and stretched it across the hall. Then Jim ran at it — and it worked! When it came to shooting the scene, Jim kept prophesying, 'It'll never work. It'll look stupid.' Of course when you see the cast hit this, their faces flatten out. You really see that when O'Neill hits it. If you watch his nose, it's all squashed against the side." A trouper to the last, Richard Dean Anderson wasn't the least bit perturbed. "I smacked right into it," he grins. "I didn't care *what* I looked like." **λ**

Above: *Go ahead, make my day. O'Neill in confrontation mode.*

Crossroads

Written by: Katharyn Powers	Guest cast: Vanessa Angel (Anise/Freya), Musetta
Directed by: Peter DeLuise	Vander (Shan'auc), Peter Wingfield (Tanith/Hebron),
	Gary Jones (Sergeant Davis), Ron Hadler (Cronus),
	Sean Millington (Ro'nak)

A n old flame of Teal'c's appears through the wormhole, claiming she can enter into two-way communication with her symbiote and gather information about the Goa'uld. Shan'auc believes the memories she has gleaned from her 'guest' could help defeat the Goa'uld, and offers to share these secrets with the Tok'ra in exchange for a willing host for her symbiote. Teal'c is initially sceptical about his former love's claims until she teaches him how to communicate with his own larvae. All seems to be going well for Shan'auc's blending until a literal snake in the grass puts an end to all her efforts.

"'Crossroads' was a great experience because we got to see a bit about Teal'c's past, that he had an unrealised love affair with Shan'auc of the Red Hills," declares Peter DeLuise. "Teal'c really struck gold there because Musetta Vander, the lady who played Shan'auc, is incredibly talented and beautiful. She played one of the henchwomen in Wild Wild West and was one of those bathing sirens in Oh Brother, Where Art Thou? But a little known secret is she was also in the running to play the part of Anise."

Obviously an actors' director, DeLuise has an instinctive feel for difficult roles and states, "Anise's was thankless dialogue. She had screeds of expositional dialogue that was so hard to pull off and make interesting. See, Amanda Tapping does that every week and makes it look easy, but every once in a while some poor actor will come on and have to do

The Tok'ra

A group of symbiote resistance fighters whose aim is to repel and destroy the evil Goa'uld and turn their race towards a less aggressive future. Although like the System Lords they require hosts, the Tok'ra do not take them by force but truly blend with them, offering the benefits of long life and health in exchange for the use of their bodies.

Above: Anise fails to notice as Shan'auc shares a smile with an old flame.

it. Not that this happened with Vanessa, but sometimes it can take up to seventeen takes to get through the crazy stuff. Goodness knows how Amanda does it — but I'd still be filming some of those scenes now if it wasn't for her skill with the crazy dialogue."

Christopher Judge had no such challenge to surmount. "I loved that episode," he crows, "because I got to kiss Musetta *all the time.*" Hastily insisting that the actress is indeed a lovely lady and a consummate professional, Judge explains, "We had a really good connection, and we had this natural competitive thing going right from morning one in the make-up trailer." Judge confesses that the time he enjoyed the most was on the last day of filming when they did the candle scene. "It starts off as me berating her, but quickly turns into her confronting me. We actually spent half a day just to shoot the juicy part of that." Unrepentant, big, tough Judge proclaims, "Listen! I could spend half the day in a clinch with Musetta Vander. Just don't tell my girlfriend." ʎ

Divide and Conquer

Written by: Tor Alexander Valenza

Directed by: Martin Wood

Guest cast: Vanessa Angel (Anise/Freya), JR Bourne (Martouf/Lantash), Kirsten Robek (Lieutenant Astor), Andrew Jackson (Supreme High Councillor Per'sus), Phillip Mitchell (Major Graham), Roger Allford (The President)

The Tok'ra High Council and the SGC are left reeling when two members of an SG team are turned into Zatarcs (programmed assassins) by Goa'uld mind control technology. With only an 'experimental' testing device likely to be able to identify potential threats, Hammond has no choice but to invite two of his most trusted veterans to undergo the perilous procedure in order to clear their names from the list. Ironically, the hidden truths revealed about Carter and O'Neill could prove damaging to their careers and their friendship, whilst Carter's mettle is pushed to the limit when she has to neutralise someone very dear to her.

O'Neill

> "I didn't leave because I'd rather die myself than lose Carter."

"What was funny about 'Divide and Conquer'," offers director Martin Wood, "was that whole Jack and Sam thing. It started in 'Solitudes' where they were cuddling up for warmth, and O'Neill had that famous line: 'It's my side arm, I swear. No Giggling.' That was the first show I did, and I loved the way they delivered that joke so much that I thought, 'We *have* to do this more often.' So, in 'Into the Fire', O'Neill goes and gets Carter, and she sits up and she's naked. When we were filming that, Rick turned to me and asked, 'Do you want this to be one of those times?' to which of course I said, 'Yes!' Then in the hallway, when they have to hide and she's too close to him, it's like, 'Wow! I am not supposed to be feeling like this.' There are a couple of really good Jack and Sam moments in other episodes, but eventually Brad and Robert decided they really had to get the 'more than colleagues' relationship out of the way. Amanda and Rick wanted it stopped too, because they were tired of skirting round that arc. A lot of the fans weren't too keen either, so we decided to knock it on the head. Rick and Amanda really loved playing that scene with the force field between them, because it's just not the sort of thing that happens on Earth. No human being, to my knowledge, has ever been forced to look at the person they love through a force field, knowing that one or

both of them is facing imminent death. I just love the way they are nose-to-nose and can't touch each other. I saw it as almost a *Midnight Express* kind of thing, you know, where the young guy is one side of the prison window and his girlfriend is on the other. Anyway, we got the whole 'feelings' thing out of the way, and I think that it was necessary and long overdue."

Above: Anise shows her gratitude in age-old fashion.

Wood is also in complete agreement with the move to kill Martouf. "That was important, because great characters have to go sometimes, just so the audience knows we mean business when we tell these stories. Even so, when I read the script I was really surprised. The fans went wild and vilify me every time they see me!" Defiant to the last, Wood exclaims, "That was not the first time I killed JR Bourne, you know. The first time I worked with him he was playing an IRA terrorist and I shot him. So the answer to 'Who shot JR?' is, 'Me — twice!'" ⅄

Window of Opportunity

Written by: Joseph Mallozzi and Paul Mullie Directed by: Peter DeLuise	Guest cast: Robin Mossley (Malikai), Dan Shea (Sergeant Siler), Daniel Bacon (Technician), Bill Nikolai (Technician), Cam Cronin (Door Airman)

Teal'c and O'Neill experience that Monday morning feeling again and again and again after a trip to another world goes disastrously wrong. The team are dispatched to explore the planet P4X639, and discover another human similarly engaged, investigating a strange alien computer. Seemingly concerned for their welfare, Malikai tells Daniel that he and his companions must leave when the atmospheric conditions begin to deteriorate, but when Daniel declines his advice, Malikai knocks him out and begins to tinker with the computer. O'Neill and Teal'c rush to help Daniel and are caught in a mysterious flash of light, only to find themselves back at SGC, ten hours earlier. As they realise that they are reliving the same events over and over again, the two men try to help the rest of their colleagues come up with a way to decode the alien machine's message, and break the time loop.

> **Teal'c**
>
> "Colonel O'Neill is right. Events do seem to be repeating themselves."

Writers Joe Mallozzi and Paul Mullie confess they had a ball writing this episode, although Mallozzi insists, "It was extremely difficult to come up with something unique, something that hadn't already been seen on *Star Trek* or any of the other sci-fi shows." Says Mullie, "We did think about pitching it seriously at one stage — but that notion didn't last long. Our background is in comedy writing. It was natural for us to resort to type."

Confirming that Mallozzi and Mullie did originally pitch it as a more serious story, executive producer Brad Wright admits, "I wasn't all that thrilled at first. I immediately thought that what we *didn't* want to do was a reprise of 'Cause and Effect', which is one of my favourite *Star Trek: The Next Generation* episodes. But Joe and Paul said, 'No! We don't want to rip off *Star Trek*. We want to rip off *Groundhog Day*!' I thought that was hilarious, and allowed them to go for it."

Wright confides, "Near the third day of shooting we knew we were going to be several minutes short. I was in kind of a panic, and suggested that we get O'Neill and Teal'c to do things they normally would never consider. I thought we should write a scene where Daniel tells them

Above: On P4X639, O'Neill means business... again.

they have the opportunity to do whatever they want, without any reper-
cussions. Hence the juggling, the golf and the kiss. The juggling came
from a need to find something they could be doing to show that they are
not listening to Daniel. Rick said, 'Hey, we could juggle. I can juggle, so
can Chris,' so off they went. All of the other little things like riding a bike
through the hallways were ideas that we all lay claim to. Rick thought of
some, the rest of us threw in suggestions too."

A keen golfer (like his colleague Chris Judge), Wright laughs, "The
golf scene came from a desire I've always had to do a long drive compe-
tition through the Stargate. Unfortunately there are no circumstances
where that could happen in a 'normal' episode without diminishing the
Stargate, but every time I went golfing, I would think about it. I am so
thankful to Joe and Paul for allowing me to realise my dream."

It's not clear whether taking Carter into his arms and swooping
down for a full blown kiss was a long-cherished desire of Colonel
O'Neill but Richard Dean Anderson grins, "I personally re-did that
scene as many times as I could get away with." Ms Tapping was not available for comment. ⅄

Watergate

Written by: Robert C. Cooper	Guest cast: Marina Sirtis (Dr Svetlana Markov), Tom
Directed by: Martin Wood	McBeath (Colonel Maybourne), Gary Jones (Sergeant
	Davis), Darryl Scheelar (Co-pilot)

Attempting their usual dial out routine, the team at Stargate Command get what is in effect a 'busy' signal that renders their Stargate unusable. SG-1 investigate and discover that the Russians have a Stargate too, hidden in a secret compound situated in the far north. But the iris is inexplicably jammed open, apparently stopping the US Stargate from functioning. Despite the fact that they will have to throw themselves out of a plane to reach the remote base, SG-1 joins an esteemed Russian scientist in an effort to reach the second Gate and close it down. Once again they find that there are more things in Heaven and Earth, and apparently, water, than can possibly be imagined.

> **Teal'c to O'Neill**
>
> "This does not seem wise, O'Neill."
>
> "I said it was easy. Not wise."

"One of the best things about 'Watergate' was we had this absolutely gorgeous location — an incredible power station," beams director Martin Wood. "We were shooting in the top part, and the next week they shot in the bottom for Peter DeLuise's show, and he kept complaining to me that we got the good part — but the entire place was tremendous." Wood also has happy memories of the C105 cargo plane they got to film in: "These guys from the United States Coast Guard flew up and said, 'Yeah! You can shoot in this thing,' and then asked if we wanted to actually go for a flight. We so wanted to do it, but didn't think our insurance would cover it, but they said, 'C'mon. It's our plane, our insurance will. Lets go.' So, all that stuff where the door opens up — that's not stock footage. That's Andy Mikita up there shooting from the back of the plane." Wood also says the shots of everybody diving out of the plane were a blast to do. "We were on the ground when that happened, and they were diving onto these huge cushions. What tickles me is Rick Anderson is the only one who actually looks like he knows how to skydive."

Wood reveals that the producers were less than confident when he said he wanted to film the mini sub from the outside, underwater. "They insisted I couldn't, because it would be too complicated and

expensive, but I had a plan. I said, 'This'll be really cool. We build a five hundred-gallon tank (it actually ended up much less than that) and we shoot through that, so it's basically a fish tank in front of the camera.' We ended up with a tank filled with clear glycerine, with an Alka Seltzer in the bottom of it so that it bubbles up in front of us. We shot a lot of the show through that." Inordinately pleased with himself and the result, Wood gives a nonchalant shrug, "Robert Cooper has this saying, 'Money plus Martin equals cool,' but John Smith is always looking at me going, 'Why do we let you stay? You cost so much money!'"

Money aside, Wood says the very, very best thing about the episode was working with guest star Marina Sirtis, the British-born actress best known for her role as Troi in that other little sci-fi show, *Star Trek: The Next Generation*. "She was lovely, and absolutely open to whatever we would bring for her to do. She has quite a cheeky sense of humour, so I wish I'd known she was a mad soccer fan when we were filming — I could have shown her a yellow card every time she answered me back!" ⋏

Above: Teal'c totters on the brink of a decision.

The First Ones

Written by: Peter DeLuise
Directed by: Peter DeLuise

Guest cast: Dion Johnstone (Chaka), Jason Schombing (Dr Robert Rothman), Vincent Hammond (Unas), Barry Levy (Major Hawkins), Steve Bacic (Major Coburn), Russell Ferrier (Captain Griff)

Dr Daniel Jackson and his former research assistant Dr Robert Rothman discover a primordial Goa'uld symbiote whilst excavating on planet P3X888, but are unable to share their discovery before a young Unas attacks the camp and makes off with an unconscious Daniel. Meanwhile, a rescue attempt by his SG-1 team mates is hampered by the fact that the water surrounding the area is alive with Goa'uld symbiotes, all looking for a host, and some of the rescue party may well have been contaminated. Working on the adage 'You never really know a person', Teal'c holds his comrades prisoner until he can determine which are threats...

Teal'c to O'Neill

"Trust me, O'Neill."

"What if I'm not O'Neill?"

"Then I was not talking to you."

Brad Wright recounts how "Peter DeLuise and I were in the back of a van out looking at locations. Peter leant over and mumbled, 'Er... Brad... I have this idea that might be fun and um... you guys can just have it 'cause I was just thinking about the show, and thought it would be cool if we went back to the place where the original Unas came from.'" Wright says, "I agreed it would be a great backdrop for a story so I told him to go ahead and write it." The executive producer jokes that for someone usually noted for his enthusiasm, DeLuise took some persuading to put the notion down on paper. "Peter kept saying, 'No! No! I'm not a writer.' But I said, 'It's a great idea so maybe you are a writer.' The outline he turned in was kind of messy, so I helped structure it for him and then insisted he carry on and write the script. I told him I wanted to mine Peter DeLuise and see what I could get out of him! Granted I rewrote the script for 'The First Ones' fairly heavily, but at its core is the script that Peter wrote, and he did a very good job of directing it."

Wright's favourite thing about the episode was the dynamic between Daniel and the young Unas, Chaka. "When you do scenes like that, you get nervous because it has all the potential to be awful. If Todd Masters hadn't done such a fabulous job on the Unas prosthetics, had

Above: Is this really a friendly Unas?

Dion Johnstone not been brilliant, and had Michael Shanks not embraced the whole friendship dynamic, it would never have worked. I loved that episode, but it was inevitably risky — right from the moment I asked Peter to write it I was nervous — so it was one of those precious little personal successes that made me, as a producer, go 'Whoo! That one worked!'"

DeLuise is flattered that the episode is a firm favourite with fans, and is delighted to hear that one of the most appealing scenes is when Daniel shares the energy bar with Chaka, and tells him it's how he met his father-in-law. "I remembered how in the original movie Daniel gives the special candy bar to Kasuf, and Erick Avari holds it like a Turkish person would hold a cigarette, then sniffs it, and finally he takes a bite of it and goes, 'Bundie — bundie way.' Now whenever Erick comes on set I always tease him by saying 'Bundie way!' every time I see him. I love that the fans like that scene; I hoped it would be something fans remembered." ⋏

Scorched Earth

Written by: Joseph Mallozzi and Paul Mullie Directed by: Martin Wood	Guest cast: Brian Markinson (Lotan), Marilyn Norry (Hedrazar), Alessandro Juliani (Eliam), Rob Court (Caleb), Nikki Smook (Nikka)

SG-1 are preparing to sit back on their laurels and revel in the fact that they have managed to transplant an endangered community, the Enkarans, from a Goa'uld slave world to a new home on a new planet. But things begin to go more than a tad awry when a gigantic alien ship appears, bent on restructuring the surface of the planet to allow the race of dormant life forms aboard the ship to re-start their lives. The members of SG-1 must face up to a moral dilemma where it appears no one member of the team can be 'right', and each one has to go their own way.

O'Neill

"We're talking about a bunch of freeze dried aliens here."

"'Scorched Earth' was our first script and is the one that actually got us our job on *Stargate*," begins Joe Mallozzi. "Considering we come from a comedy base, this is quite a departure for Paul and myself as it's a very serious, issue-driven piece where the members of SG-1 are forced to follow their own path as to where they stand on the moral dilemma posed." Mullie offers, "It comes right down to a question of who has the right to live. The people transplanted there by SG-1, who are a relatively small group of living, breathing individuals, or the thousands of DNA samples ready to resurrect an entire civilisation?" Thankfully a satisfactory solution is found but the episode did pose some serious questions for everyone involved. Martin Wood comments, "We spent a lot of time discussing script points with this episode. Richard Dean Anderson, for instance, wasn't comfortable with the fact that O'Neill does things Richard did not believe in, and was reluctant to portray."

Not only were the actors tortured over their responses to the questions posed by the script, Martin Wood tested the mettle of actress Marilyn Norry during 'Scorched Earth'. He says, "She is meant to be going blind in the episode so I had her fitted with contact lenses, and she really couldn't see a thing. She was absolutely terrific about it, but it did put her in an extremely vulnerable position, so anytime anyone went up to her they had to be very gentle and explain who they were and what they wanted to talk about, so she could turn her head in the right direction."

Above: Sam and Daniel review the latest CD ROMs.

Talking of turning heads, in the scene where Daniel Jackson and the robot Lotan are wandering down a tree-lined avenue, careful viewers will see that they sneak the odd look back along the path they've just walked down. The looks weren't for dramatic effect, they were for self-preservation. "To everyone's total amazement a bear just came lumbering out of the woods as we started shooting," gasps the director. "Most of us stayed pretty calm; we sent the grips out to coax it away, but our resident tough guy — Christopher Judge — who is a bit of an urban alien who doesn't get to see much wildlife, took to his trailer and wouldn't come out! Michael and Brian, however, had to get on and do the scene. Hence the shifty looks backwards every now and then to see if the bear was back."

Not everything about the episode was quite as terrifying, however. Executive producer Michael Greenburg has happier memories. His girlfriend Nikki Smook was chosen to play the expecting Enkaran Nikka, as she really *was* heavily pregnant. A short time after the episode was completed, baby Kenya made her first appearance. λ

Beneath the Surface

Written by: Heather E. Ash
Directed by: Peter DeLuise

Guest cast: Alison Matthews (Brenna), Kim Hawthorne (Kegan), Laurie Murdock (Administrator Calder), Russell Ferrier (Major Griff)

There's not a lot of 'Hi-ho, hi-ho' when SG-1 are sent to work in the mines beneath the surface of an apparently ice-covered planet. With memories of their former lives dismissed as mere dreams, O'Neill, Carter, Daniel and Teal'c are now called Jonah, Therra, Carlin and Tor, doomed to a mundane and miserable life as labourers. Even Carter/Therra's attempt to improve the efficiency and safety of their conditions is thwarted by unscrupulous leaders. Unaware that General Hammond is trying to unravel the mystery of their disappearance, the four that were once SG-1 form a natural bond, pooling fragments of memory to rebuild a picture of their former lives and forge an escape plan.

> **O'Neill**
>
> "SG-1? What kind of a name is that for a team?"

Peter DeLuise reiterates that he managed to pull off his usual stroke of filling the scenes with big, sweaty guys and loads of dirt: "Yes, 'Beneath the Surface' was one of my successes there!" Asked whether the infamous 'Homer' line was scripted or the result of an ad lib, the director replies, "I will tell you that it was definitely scripted. It was not an ad lib, and because of the far reaching implications it was done in two different scenes. Whenever I speak to fans, it seems to me that they think the writing happens magically, and all the funny bits are improvised by the actors. Because it's their faces that are on screen, they get the credit for a lot of the really good writing that goes on."

Paul Mullie and Joe Mallozzi smile, "We wrote the joke where O'Neill is describing a memory to Carter and he says, 'There's a man who's very important to me. He's bald and he wears a short sleeved shirt. I think his name is Homer.' We actually wrote 'Homer Simpson' but Brad Wright thought it would be funnier if it was just Homer." There was a lot of deliberation, but the writers agree that Wright made the right decision.

A bit of a giggler himself, DeLuise is impressed that Richard Dean Anderson and Amanda Tapping managed to carry off the scene and keep a straight face long enough to commit it to celluloid. "They are very professional, but I could show you *hours and hours* of footage which is ruined by Richard being funny and Amanda laughing."

Tapping can testify to that. "We all love *The Simpsons*, Rick especially, and there were a lot of Homer references in that episode. Normally we try to get the laughter out during rehearsal, because when we start rolling suddenly you're under so much pressure because film is being used and it's costing money. But Rick is the worst person on our crew for this — he'll turn and give you a little twinkle in his eye just before you start, and you're completely lost. Or he'll turn his back to the camera so they can't see what he's doing and he'll just give you this little smile, and I've gone." Peter DeLuise swears, "I love Rick's humour and his dry wit. It's a real thrill to work with someone like that and it's such a luxury to have it on a show that doesn't take itself too seriously." Å

Above: Teal'c withstands the heat in the kitchen.

Point of No Return

Written by: Joseph Mallozzi and Paul Mullie Directed by: William Gereghty	Guest cast: Willie Garson (Martin Lloyd), Robert Lewis (Dr Peter Tanner), Matthew Bennett (Ted), Mar Andersons (Bob), Francis Boyle (Sergeant Peters)

Hammond receives a taped message from one Martin Lloyd, who claims to have information on all manner of 'government conspiracies' from the Kennedy cover-up to more recent examples. He's dismissed as a crackpot until he outlines details of the Stargate programme, so SG-1 goes undercover to investigate the man and find out where he's getting his information. First impressions would seem to indicate that Marty, who insists he's a displaced alien, is nothing more than a paranoid delusional. However, events reveal he may not be as crazy as the team first thought, and that he may indeed have come from outer space...

Daniel Jackson

"I've never been on a stakeout before. Shouldn't we have doughnuts?"

As some people reading this may be aware, Joseph Mallozzi is a great fan of the Internet, and can often be found lurking (or even interacting) with fans on the World Wide Web (when he and partner Paul Mullie aren't slaving away writing their episodes of *Stargate SG-1* that is).

So it comes as no surprise when he says, "The idea for 'Point of No Return' grew out of the fact that there are lots of websites out there where the participants believe there is an actual Stargate programme, and that the show is a cover-up for what is really happening." Paul Mullie adds, "We love that kind of rationale, and wanted to play around with that idea, so we went with the notion that our characters become involved with someone who thinks he knows the truth about the Stargate, who turns out to be an alien who can only get home through the Gate."

Although Mallozzi feels the episode is interesting because the characters get out into the real world of today, get to wear regular clothes and interact with regular human beings (for the most part), he does give a sigh of relief that he and Mullie managed to incorporate a Stargate into the episode. It may only have been for a few scant seconds at the end, but at least it was there: "We'd written two or three episodes all of which took place on Earth and the producers

Above: Martin Lloyd points to an underground conspiracy.

eventually said to us, 'Guys, you do know the Stargate goes off-world, don't you?' We really wanted to stay with this show, so we kind of pandered to that thought," Mallozzi grins.

Richard Dean Anderson advises, "Working with Willie Garson [the actor perhaps now better known for his recurring role as Stanford Blatch in the series *Sex and the City*] is an experience everyone should have. Working with him is an absolute joy, and I wish he were a regular on the show so I could work with him all the time. He is one of the funniest human beings on the face of the planet and is wonderful just to be around, let alone work with. When we put him back in for our 100th episode [season five's hilarious 'Wormhole X-Treme!'] it made me very happy. I adore him." ⋋

Tangent

Written by: Michael Cassutt	Guest cast: Carmen Argenziano (Jacob Carter/Selmak),
Directed by: Peter DeLuise	Colin Cunningham (Major Davis), Peter Williams (Apophis), Steven Williams (General Vidrine)

T eal'c and O'Neill are delighted to show off the prowess of the X-301, an experimental craft created from the remains of a pair of captured Goa'uld Death Gliders. Sadly, the planned showcase flight goes awry and the two team mates go hurtling into outer space. An attempt is made to alter the ship's course and head it back in the direction of Earth but when this fails, it's up to Daniel, Carter and the Tok'ra to effect a rescue. Helplessly travelling further and further away from 'home', Teal'c and O'Neill must conserve every ounce of energy to have any chance of surviving their ordeal.

Brad Wright begins, "I quite enjoyed this episode for what it was. Michael Cassutt gave me my first job on *The Outer Limits* so it was a little bit of payback. It was another one that I rewrote completely because the original script could not be produced, but the goal was to do our version of *Apollo 13*. What I really loved about that episode, aside from the fabulous visual effects, was Richard Dean Anderson's embracing of the role of astronaut. If you look at his performance it's quite studied. He took the role of a pilot in a perilous situation in a spacecraft very seriously, and I think he proves himself to be a grown-up actor. The thing I love about Rick is that as irreverent as he can be when he plays O'Neill, when it's time to get serious he does so. He's not a goof all of the time, and sometimes I think our fans don't give him enough credit for knowing when to be wacky and when not to be."

Peter DeLuise shares Wright's enthusiasm for the performance from the two men trapped in the ship: "The situation had plenty of potential to be boring — two guys sitting in a cockpit — they couldn't even see each other. I thought the way they played the two guys dying slowly was incredible. As they become more and more oxygen deprived, we see the subtleties of their characters, their layers, their vulnerability. When Teal'c compliments O'Neill for his friendship and O'Neill replies, 'Right back atcha', I don't think you could beat it for poignancy."

Brad Wright also mentions an interesting side note: "I thought it was hilarious that I got vilified by some fans who thought a person would explode if they were exposed to a vacuum, and told me so in no uncertain terms. What was even more fun was that smarter and more informed and more educated fans came rushing to my defence by saying that what we wrote for *Stargate* was technically more accurate. They posted messages on the Internet saying, 'You don't immediately freeze to death and you don't immediately explode. That's just what happens in the movies.' Now I'm not saying we don't bend the truth a little, but we do try to have some sense of specifics. It's cool that people recognise that." λ

Above: O'Neill is very lost in space.

Serpent's Venom

Written by: Peter DeLuise
Directed by: Martin Wood

Guest cast: Carmen Argenziano (Jacob Carter/Selmak), Obi Ndefo (Rak'nor), Paul Koslo (Terok), Peter Williams (Apophis), Douglas H. Arthurs (Heru-ur), Art Kitching (Ma'kar)

Teal'c's life literally hangs in the balance when he is captured during a mission to his home planet of Chulak. Instead of drumming up support for a Jaffa rebellion, he is hauled off and tortured by minions of the System Lord Heru-ur. Unaware of his predicament, the rest of SG-1 teams up with Jacob Carter in an effort to stop an alliance between Apophis and Heru-ur coming to fruition. Whilst trying to stay in one piece amidst a floating minefield, the team realise that the stakes are even higher when they find that the gift Heru-ur brings to seal the deal is none other than Teal'c.

> **O'Neill to Carter**
>
> "Do you understand any of that?"
>
> "It's all Phoenician to me, sir."

Christopher Judge maintains he sported bruises sustained during the course of that episode for weeks. "Martin Wood directed 'Serpent's Venom' and he's always open to actors' suggestions," Judge begins, wincing even before he tells the story. "Now, I'm not really a method actor, but in this case I thought it would help my performance if I was actually in a state of discomfort. So those scenes where I'm hanging from the chains — there is no harness there. I'm actually hanging by those little cuffs and *man*, were they biting into me. They were very uncomfortable, but they helped me achieve what I was trying to show. Of course, I had to have lots of TLC afterwards to make up for my ordeal."

Heru-ur

Also known as Horus the Elder, Heru-ur is purported to be the offspring of Ra and Hathor. However, if that were true, he would be Harsesis and therefore able to use the combined knowledge of the Goa'uld against others to become the dominant power in the universe. More likely to be the adopted son of Ra, Heru-ur has tried to steal the son of Apophis and Ammonet/Sha're in order to obtain the all-important information carried within the boy.

Above: The torturer Terok in action.

According to Judge, the actor Paul Koslo, who played Terok, the man sent to torture Teal'c in the episode, scared the Hell out of everyone from the minute he turned up at the audition. "Martin told me the story of how when Paul did his audition scene, it was so fantastic that no one could tell if he was acting or if he was really crazy. Everyone was so freaked they sent Martin out afterwards to talk to him."

Teasing that the producers were working on the basis that it 'takes one to know one', Judge hoots, "They sent Martin to decipher if the guy was really a nutcase or just capable of turning in a great performance!" Similarly, the actor's first meeting with the guest star caused a twinge of concern: "The first rehearsal was my first meeting with him and he came to set wholly in character and I went up to Martin and said, 'This dude's crazy!' That's when he told me the audition story. After rehearsal the guy and I talked and he turned out to be a very lovely man." λ

The Curse

Written by: Joseph Mallozzi and Paul Mullie
Directed by: Andy Mikita

Guest cast: Anna-Louise Plowman (Sarah Gardner), Ben Bass (Dr Steven Rayner), David Abbott (Dr David Jordan), Lorena Gale (Curator), Dan Shea (Sergeant Siler)

D aniel Jackson is disturbed to read that his former professor has been killed in a mysterious lab explosion. He returns to his Alma Mater for the funeral and meets up with some of his former colleagues, not all of whom are glad to see him. Daniel discovers that the professor was studying an ancient Egyptian jar which just happened to contain the preserved remains of a Goa'uld symbiote. Alarmed to find out that a second jar has gone missing and that a Goa'uld could be on the loose, Daniel enlists the help of Sam Carter and Janet Fraiser to unravel the mystery. Meanwhile, Teal'c accompanies O'Neill on a *very* challenging mission.

> **Teal'c**
>
> "We have caught nothing. We are fishing."

"I played a lot of golf during that episode," confirms Christopher Judge. "Standing watching O'Neill not catching any fish was not the highlight of the time I've spent on *Stargate SG-1*, but it was fun to play the humour thing to the full."

There was much humour off set too. Teryl Rothery giggles as she recalls the wardrobe requirements that inspired a new pair of *alter egos*: "I became Turtle to Amanda's Gazelle because, as you know, I am fairly petite and was wearing this huge back-pack and this little baseball cap and I came rushing in and Amanda said, 'Wow! You look just like a turtle.' Once we'd stopped laughing I asked her what animal she would be most likely to represent and without missing a beat we both yelled out 'a gazelle' and it

Osiris Jars

These Egyptian artefacts were discovered in 1931 and allegedly contained the remains of Isis and Osiris. The inscriptions on the jars read, 'Woe to all who disturb this, my final resting place' — a curse that seems to have afflicted many of those who have handled them. Every member of the original expedition died within a year of finding the artefacts, and the ship carrying them sank. The mysterious deaths of those associated with the jars occur to this day.

Above: The newly awakened Osiris is not in a good mood.

stuck. So now, not only do we joke about pretending to be Charlene and Minnie — two Southern belle beauty students — we are Turtle and Gazelle as well!'"

Amanda Tapping says they were torn between laughter and screams as Michael Shanks drove them across the sand dunes that were meant to represent the Egyptian desert. "We were in an open jeep-type thing, and Michael drove like a bat out of Hell. We were bouncing around and clinging on for dear life, not sure whether to laugh like banshees or scream like girlies. We were worried about rolling over but the safety guys just yelled, 'Just keep your arms in, you'll be fine.'" Happily, no actors were harmed in the making of this episode.

Always one to support black actors in leading roles, Christopher Judge comments, "Usually I complain that every time we see an Egyptian goddess in the show, she's played by a white woman when historically that's not always accurate. But with Anna-Louise Plowman I didn't mind at all because not only is she a great actress, she has this remarkable bearing and presence. She's so calm and controlled and has a quality of stillness that is very tangible when you're around her. She was the perfect choice." λ

Chain Reaction

Written by: Joseph Mallozzi and Paul Mullie **Directed by:** Martin Wood	Guest cast: Lawrence Dane (General Bauer), Tom McBeath (Colonel Maybourne), Ronny Cox (Senator Kinsey)

T hings take a turn for the worst for the SG-1 team when General Hammond makes the surprise announcement that he is retiring. O'Neill protests that there is no way Hammond was likely to do that voluntarily, but the General refuses to support the accusation and leaves his most respected team in the hands of one General Bauer. Carter is immediately re-assigned and ordered to construct a planet-killing Naquadah bomb. Daniel and Teal'c are seriously demoted and demoralised. It's left to O'Neill to try to restore the status quo, but to do so he must seek assistance from a most unlikely ally.

> **Teal'c**
>
> "On Chulak, when a great warrior retires from the field of battle it is customary to sing a song of lament. Fortunately we are not on Chulak."

Brad Wright is full of praise for the two newest team writers, saying, "'Chain Reaction' was a gem of a script by Paul Mullie and Joe Mallozzi, furthering the NID conspiracy storyline. It became obvious in season one that big epic adventures may be fan favourites, but with the limited budgets and time restrictions of television, we needed to create engaging storylines on Earth that had few visual effects or grandiose sets." Wright also reveals that the episode gave him an opportunity to cast Larry Dane as a guest star. "He and Don were the only two actors Jonathan Glassner and I originally considered for Hammond, having worked with both men in *The Outer Limits*. It was great to see Ronny Cox return as Senator Kinsey in that episode, too."

Having pipped Lane at the post for promotion to General, Don S. Davis feels 'Chain Reaction' is one of the episodes that gave him the opportunity to show the inner strength and moral commitment of Hammond: "One of the things I admire most about the character is that he knows how to play by the rules, but isn't afraid to question or stand up to them if need be. He is not the type of man to kowtow to anyone just because the rule book says he should. As a dedicated military man, resigning from the United States Air Force was one of the hardest things he's had to do. However, the circumstances in which he found himself left Hammond no choice. He would not allow him-

Above: Right a bit, left a bit. Fire! Carter builds a Naquadah planet-killer.

self to become a pawn for a government agency that wanted to take over the SGC for some nefarious purpose and took the necessary but, in his mind, totally appropriate action."

Director Martin Wood enjoys telling the story of how he made the malicious Maybourne eat lots of hotdogs, but location manager Lynn Smith remembers a few other people taking advantage of the fast food: "We hired a hotdog vendor to be in that scene but we fell a bit behind in our shooting schedule. By the time we got around to using him, he had already started selling his wares to anyone who happened to stray onto the beach, which wasn't quite what we had in mind."

They say every dog has his or, in this case, her day — and 'Chain Reaction' gave Zoe the chance to shine. If it looked as though 'Oscar' the dog was delighted to see Colonel O'Neill, it was quite possibly because, after his daughter Wylie of course, Zoe is the other girl in Richard Dean Anderson's life! ⋏

Written by: Brad Wright	Guest cast: Christopher Cousins (Joe), Dion Luther
Directed by: Andy Mikita	(Mollem), Gary Jones (Sergeant Davis), Ronny Cox
	(President Kinsey)

t's ten years hence and the world is a very different place. Carter is married to an ambassador, Daniel Jackson is a well-respected scientist, Teal'c has lost his tattoo and O'Neill has gone fishing. An apparently benign super race called the Aschen has taken Earth under its wing; providing the technology and wherewithal to defeat not just the Goa'uld but life threatening diseases as well. It seems that almost everyone on the planet is delighted with the benefits bestowed by these 'friends', though one or two people still have doubts. Then Janet Fraiser discovers that Sam and Joe's inability to conceive a child is the result of direct interference by the Aschen, whilst O'Neill reveals that he never trusted them. As the other members of the former SG-1 realise the world is in grave danger, they must return to the past to safeguard the future.

Carter

"The Aschen can control planets. You don't think they can control the media?"

Allowing himself a very small pat on the back Brad Wright offers, "'2010' is my favourite *Stargate*. It's my best work and though I write a lot of the stuff that doesn't have my name on it, you can be sure that if something *does* have my name on the writer credits it's going to be something that hasn't been done before, in episodic television at least." Wright was particularly pleased with the scenes between Sam and Joe, and Carter and O'Neill. "Amanda got nominated for a Gemini award for her performance in that episode, and I always take a little quiet pride when an actor gets nominated for something I wrote."

"That was a big episode for me," Amanda Tapping states. "I'm married to someone other than Jack, and I thought it was great that ten years on Carter has moved forward with a guy that is not Colonel O'Neill. And she is happily married, they are really in love with each other. As a person, I loved the fact that I got to wear clothes other than army boots, that I was struggling with not being able to have children, and that there was still tension between O'Neill and me that seemed almost to be manifesting itself in hostility toward each other. I remember filming that one scene where I'm at the cabin begging for his help. Originally it was written that he storms off and leaves me on his front lawn, but I went up to

the director and said that it made more sense for *me* to storm off, because I am the one who's moved on and I need to leave again. So they let me do it, and I basically got to say, 'Well, fine. Have it your way. This is why I never married you, you stubborn little boy.' I loved that."

Above: Teal'c, Sam and Daniel salute an absent friend.

Tapping shares another of her favourite moments by recounting what happened during the final Gallipoli-like scene. "We did the episode shortly after *Galaxy Quest* came out, and we were shooting the final scene where Rick comes flying down on that big rope and gets hit by the lasers. I was watching him in rehearsal and he gets hit and does this roll, reminiscent of Tim Allen's in the film at the bit where Alan Rickman turns to him and says 'Is that absolutely necessary?' I turned to Andy Mikita and repeated those words along with 'What next? Is he going to lose his shirt?' We were falling about laughing. On the actual take, I gathered the whole crew round the set and the monitors and when Andy calls 'Action', Rick comes propelling down, hits the ground and all of a sudden you hear the entire crew making laser sounds. He had to carry on whilst the rest of us were laughing like drains. Poor Rick!" λ

Absolute Power

Written by: Robert C. Cooper
Directed by: Peter DeLuise

Guest Cast: Lane Gates (Shifu), Peter Williams (Apophis), Colin Cunningham (Major Davis), Gary Jones (Sergeant Davis), William de Vry (Aldwin), Erick Avari (Kasuf), Steven Williams (General Vidrine)

S G-1 returns to Abydos and encounters a swirling sandstorm which twists itself out to reveal a young boy. Introducing himself as Shifu, the Harsesis, he allows Daniel to take him back to Stargate Command for tests. Although it appears Shifu is a perfectly normal and healthy child, spiritually and intellectually he is wise beyond his years. As he also possesses all the knowledge of the Goa'uld and could, therefore, prove to be the instrument of their downfall, the boy decides to gift Daniel with all the genetic memories he holds. What Daniel chooses to do with such power is for him alone to decide…

Shifu

"Questions are plentiful. Answers are few."

Robert Cooper offers, "Many of the stories I've written come from a personal desire to fill holes that I think develop from time to time in the series' ever-evolving mythology. I blame no one. Often it is I who have created the hole in the first place! We had often talked about 'all the knowledge of the Goa'uld' and about how getting some of it would help us defeat them. For once, I wanted to get a taste of what that knowledge was. The thing that attracted Brad and I to the story was the idea that this Goa'uld knowledge could not be had in the form of raw data, and that the only form in which it *could* be had would corrupt us to the point of destruction. The Goa'uld seemed to be born evil. The genetic knowledge they inherit is so intertwined with awful memories that it cannot help but make them twisted. Only Oma Desala's power protected the Harsesis from its effects. It would be interesting to see what would happen to someone not so protected."

The writer goes on to say, "When we were coming up with the story, Brad, as he often does, got obsessively hooked on a particular image. In this case, it was that of the boy arriving in the desert in the form of a twister. VFX superhero James Tichenor was reluctant, because the effect was going to be very expensive and he wasn't sure it was going to work in the end. James will tell you that this was one of the many times I've made him sick to his stomach as I force him to try a very costly

effect that both of us know could be disastrous. This one turned out great. Brad got his twister and was very happy."

The episode also boasts one of the writer's favourite sets: Daniel's mission control. "It was quite simple really. Lots of video screens, some black backgrounds and a really cool chair. It created a bit of a panic during prep though, as we realised there would have to be something playing back on each one of the screens and there were dozens of them!"

Many fans have wondered how lovely, sweet Daniel Jackson could turn into such a nasty person so quickly. Michael Shanks has the answer: "He never was a bad person; he was the same Daniel all the way through the episode, we just saw him in a different set of circumstances. We all know that when Daniel is on the track of something he gets really passionate and adamant about what he thinks he can accomplish. This was Daniel being himself, and it was important to Robert Cooper and to me that we not tip the hand of what he was up to until the very end — that we perceive him as a bad person finally because we see the results of the process." ⋏

Above: Daniel ponders whether to have breakfast or destroy a chunk of the western world.

The Light

| Written by: James Phillips | Guest cast: Kristian Ayre (Loran), Gary Jones |
| Directed by: Peter F. Woeste | (Sergeant Davis), Link Baker (Lieutenant Barber) |

Near death, Daniel Jackson returns from a mission to a remote off-world temple. One member of another SG unit has committed suicide, and two others are in a bad way. It's up to the remainder of SG-1 to find out what has caused this apparently incurable condition. They visit the temple and discover a bright, mesmerising light that sends anyone within close range into a heightened state of euphoria. Unfortunately, this addictive pleasure also inflicts severe withdrawal symptoms on anyone attempting to leave the light's corona. Drawn likes moths to a flame, the team's only hope of breaking away lies with a young boy found wandering around the abandoned site.

Daniel to O'Neill

"This thing isn't working."

"Did you check the batteries?"

Although many would agree that Michael Shanks was totally convincing as the mentally and physiologically disturbed archaeologist in this episode, Shanks himself takes a more pragmatic view: "It was one of those things where, when you do a character for a long time, particularly over four seasons, I had done so much with Daniel and played so many of those types of scenes that, to be honest, I was kind of over it. Just the previous season in 'Legacy' I had played a similar suicidal-type Daniel in a similar-type situation. In 'Need' the season before that, the confrontation was exactly the same, where he wanted to do something drastic and Jack had to talk him down. It was almost literally the same

The Light

An ultimately destructive device created by the Goa'uld for visitors to their rest and recreation palace — similar to an Opium den — on planet P4X347. A battery-powered pedestal, which houses the device's components, projects a highly seductive light-matrix hologram on to the ceiling and surrounding area. The intense colours and bright light trigger chemical responses in the brain that are initially pleasing and soporific. Exposure for even a short time results in addiction, leading to increasingly aggressive behaviour and severe depression when the subject is removed from the source.

thing, so for me with 'The Light', it was more of a challenge to try to find a different way to do that same kind of scene than it was to actually do the journey."

Above: SG-1 *discover what the Goa'uld do for pleasure.*

An actor who always analyses every facet of his performance, as Shanks puts it, "to the nth degree", he wishes he had had the time to do more with that particular scenario. "In 'Legacy' and 'Need' I had an entire episode where we watched that arc, where we watched Daniel unravel, so to speak. In 'The Light' I think I had about the first ten minutes of the episode. Even though I had done it before I really didn't want to do it the same way, obviously, so it became one of those situations where I was whining to the producers: 'I've already done this. Why don't you get one of the other actors to do it?'" Clearly recognising the man's talents, Shanks was persuaded with the view, "But you do it so well." However, he still maintains it was one of his bigger challenges. "It was incredibly tough trying to find a way to inject new life into that type of arc given the confines of the process and the short period of time to get the point across." All credit to Shanks for undoubtedly succeeding. ᛉ

Prodigy

Story by: Brad Wright, Joseph Mallozzi and Paul Mullie Teleplay by: Joseph Mallozzi and Paul Mullie Directed by: Peter DeLuise	Guest cast: Elisabeth Rosen (Cadet Jennifer Hailey), Hrothgar Mathews (Dr Hamilton), Bill Dow (Dr Lee), General Ryan (Himself), Keith Martin Gordey (Professor Munroe), Michael Kopsa (General Kerrigan), Roger Haskett (Dr Bill Thompson)

When Sam Carter meets the strong-willed, rebellious Jennifer Hailey, she sees much of herself in the young cadet, and is eager to encourage the development of the younger woman's potential. Cadet Hailey, on the other hand, is fed up with rules, regulations and being constantly compared to the brilliant astrophysicist. Carter decides the best course of action might be to take the cadet on a trip through the Stargate to give her a taste of what's to come should she rein in her temper and independent streak. However, the routine mission to an off-world research base turns into a battle of life and death when a swarm of deadly life forms turn against SG-1 and the group of scientists they are protecting.

> **Hailey to Carter**
>
> "Is it always like this?"
>
> "Sometimes it gets quite exciting."

"'Prodigy' started with the desire to bring the Academy into *Stargate*, as in showing where the new recruits came from," begins Brad Wright. "But it was one of those attempts at starting a new thread that I probably won't continue with. I kind of wanted to create a new character, but sometimes these things just don't work out. I also thought it would be a fairly simple, under-patterned story. You know, one of those cheaper episodes that we do to pay for the bigger ones, but those little glowing aliens — you would not *believe* how expensive they were! If I'd known, I might never even have told their story." Disgusted at the amount of money thrown at something so tiny, Wright takes some solace in the set and the script: "Richard Hudolin did a fabulous job of the set, and that episode has some of my favourite jokes in it. The bit where Teal'c says, 'I am going to shoot you O'Neill' then floors him always makes me laugh."

Amanda Tapping remembers, "Michael Shanks was supposed to direct that episode which I was really excited about, because one of the two very distinct stories in that episode was based around me, and we had had long chats about how to play those moments. Circumstances

meant that we had to change directors at the last moment and fortunately it became Peter DeLuise, who did a great job anyway." The actress says, "I think we fell short in that episode on the Carter/Hailey side. We had the potential to tell a story about the nature of genius and how volatile that is, and how you deal with it. There are geniuses who have no social skills whatsoever, there are all kinds of angles you can play about what it means to be a genius, but I don't think we explored that to the full."

Above: Carter and Cadet Hailey in accord, for once.

That said, Tapping does acknowledge they only had forty minutes of television to tell two distinct and different stories. "The premise of the Cadet Hailey arc was wonderful, though. I like that whole side of going back to the Academy, and it was a shame that we didn't have enough time to explore Hailey in more depth. If we had, we would have been able to see that her anger and frustration was borne out of having too much information in her head with no direction in which to really focus it. Elizabeth Rosen played Hailey with this edge, this stillness and that chip on her shoulder, which is ironic because in real life (and she won't mind me saying this) she is a real goof!" ⋏

Entity

Written by: Peter DeLuise	Guest cast: Gary Jones (Sergeant Davis), Dan Shea
Directed by: Allan Lee	(Sergeant Siler)

The tables are turned when an innocent surveillance probe is perceived as a catastrophic threat and an alien race returns a more deadly device to infect the computers at the SGC, bringing doom, gloom and chaos. Detected early, the entity manages to escape deletion by using the electrical circuit in the MALP room to survive and grow. Once it is discovered, Sam Carter tries to communicate with it in order to find out if some sort of compromise can be achieved, but her attempt results in the entity growing ever stronger, now within Carter's own body. Hammond is left with the agonising dilemma of whether to sacrifice one of his own in order to save the base.

Peter DeLuise came up with the idea for 'Entity' because, he thought, "It would be great to deal with the consequences of a 'consciousness in the machine' concept, but where the damage being done to our side was as a result of another race's self-preservation. You know — we send out one of our routine probes but the very signal we're sending is hurting the aliens horribly so they return a death probe to stop us doing it. I thought having the antagonist acting for some noble cause would make the story a little more interesting." Incidentally, DeLuise remarks that the electronic voice used by Carter was an homage to Amanda Tapping's hero, the real life scientist Professor Stephen Hawking.

Given her naturally bubbly nature, portraying a still, bed-ridden Carter was a major challenge for Amanda Tapping: "It was a really difficult episode for all sorts of reasons. First off it was so *not* Carter. This woman was so still and so angry and so dark. Considering I spent most of the time in bed, I was exhausted at the end of that episode. I had to book myself into the spa for a month to recover," she jokes.

"I also found it quite hard to buy into the story, and these are the times when as an actor you just have to acquiesce to your character and say, 'OK. I'll just have to become Carter 110 percent and react to this situation as she would without analysing it as Amanda.' You just have to relax and give everything over to your character. The

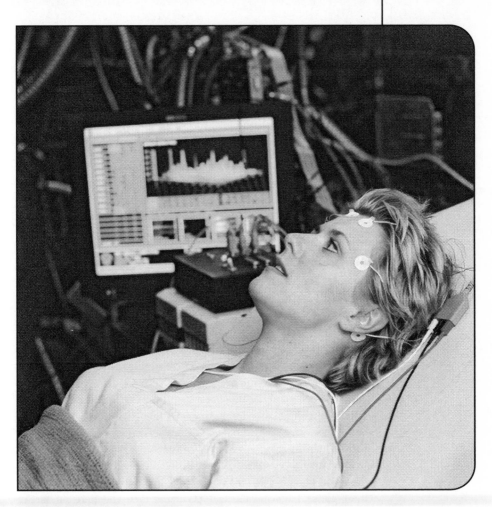

beauty of it is having this great challenge of playing a very different Carter. All I did was lie in bed twitching, or else I sat and stared at people the whole episode. It was terribly difficult." She winks, "You have no idea."

The actress also reveals that the entire cast and crew were very nervous the whole time because they were using new technology to shoot the episode. "We shot it digitally, which is a really difficult medium. We'd stuck to 35mm for a while, so there was a lot of weirdness because using digital cameras changes the way you shoot. We were trying to get used to and compensate for that. Suffice it to say that it was the first and last time we've ever shot on digital!" ⅄

Above: Carter, suffering from an overdose of alien technology.

Double Jeopardy

Written by: Robert C. Cooper	Guest cast: Belinda Waymouth (Goa'uld officer), Jay
Directed by: Michael Shanks	Brazeau (Harlan), Ron Halder (Cronus), Matthew
	Harrison (Darian), Bill Croft (Sindar)

D aniel Jackson loses his head and Harlan returns to the SGC with a much subdued 'Comtrya' and a plea for SG-1 to go help 'themselves'. The robot SG team created by Harlan has been travelling through their Stargate in much the same way as their human counterparts, only this time trouble has finally caught up with them. Trapped and tortured on an alien planet they once freed from Goa'uld tyranny, time is slipping away from both SG-1 teams who must battle against the snakeheads, the locals and the clock in order to defeat the vengeful Cronus.

Harlan

"It's a very big emergency. You must help you."

Whilst it seemed to take forever to come together, Robert C. Cooper is delighted with the way this episode turned out: "We had been trying to come up with a sequel to 'Tin Man' for a long time. Three years to be exact. There were many versions. We knew we wanted the robots out there doing what SG-1 did — exploring the galaxy. At one point, we thought we wanted SG-1 to have to save them from a difficult situation but the more we thought about it, the more we didn't know why SG-1 would get involved. Then we decided the robots had to help *us* solve a problem, and possibly give their lives in the process. That gave us the structure. Besides the great character of Harlan the robot, the thing that made 'Tin Man' interesting was the twist. You think you're following the real SG-1 and then you find out they're mechanical. I wanted to see if I could pull off the exact same twist again without making it feel cheap." The writer admits there were challenges. "Time has passed: hairstyles, weapons, uniforms etc would all be hints to the regular viewer that something was going on and we knew we couldn't keep it up for long. That's why the Daniel robot was beheaded in act two. From there, we knew it would be fun to have the robots and the real SG-1 reluctantly working together."

The episode was not without some challenges behind the camera. "Michael Shanks was supposed to get a nice easy episode to direct for his first time in the big chair," Cooper continues. "A scheduling nightmare made that impossible and we realised 'Double Jeopardy' was going to fall

on his spot. It was one of the biggest shows we had ever attempted to produce. There was action, locations, huge sets and twinning [time consuming, complicated VFX involving multiple characters played by the same actor in the same shot]. I think Michael thought it was my revenge for all those times he wouldn't say the lines I had written for him. It wasn't intentional. (Just an added bonus.) In the end, the episode turned out as good as it could have, and Michael did a solid job under difficult circumstances."

Above: Pride doth cometh before a fall. Cronus's finest hour.

Asked how difficult it was working with 'himself', Richard Dean Anderson grins, "Well I work with myself all the time. Technically, 'Double Jeopardy' was difficult because you shoot two sides of a scene so it's technologically work intensive. The rest of it was easy and fun because I could take liberties with myself as an actor that I can't necessarily take with other actors who don't really know where I'm coming from. However," he adds, not entirely seriously, "most of the time, *I* don't know where I'm coming from, so that complicates matters. But when I had scenes with myself it was fun. I actually prefer it!" λ

Exodus

Written by: Joseph Mallozzi and Paul Mullie **Directed by:** David Warry-Smith	**Guest cast:** Carmen Argenziano (Jacob Carter/Selmak), Peter Wingfield (Tanith), Peter Williams (Apophis), Malik McCall (First Guard), Kenton Reid (Red Jaffa), Paul Norman (Apophis's Red Guard)

This time it's SG-1's turn to arrive bearing gifts for the Tok'ra. They arrive at their home world of Vorash on Cronus's mothership with the intention of lending it to the Tok'ra long enough to facilitate a move to a safer planet. However, Tanith, one of the high council members, is less than happy that he was not informed of the plan — but he is silenced when his compatriots reveal that they know of his duplicity and continued loyalty to Apophis. Tanith escapes from custody and lets Apophis know of the Tok'ra's intentions. The System Lord assembles his fleet and arrives at Vorash to wipe the planet off the face of the galaxy. Unfortunately for SG-1, their plan to use Apophis's arrogance against him goes awry, and the team once more finds itself adrift without a rudder, far, far from home.

> **O'Neill**
>
> "This is so the last time I help someone move."

Robert C. Cooper is in characteristic jovial mood when asked to supply some recollections associated with this episode. Joking that his main memory was what he had for lunch that week, he informs us, "Lox and cream cheese on a bagel with a side of tuna and some cut up vegetables. It was very nice." Thank you Mr Cooper. Realising readers would probably like a bit more detail pertaining to the actual episode he goes on: "'Exodus' was our big season finale. It was written by Joe [Mallozzi] and Paul [Mullie] and produced by yours truly. David Warry-Smith did an amazing job of directing it. It was a real cliffhanger of a story in which SG-1 lend the Tok'ra their newly acquired mothership and get into trouble with Apophis's approaching fleet. It was truly massive on the visual effects side; we even blow up a star in this one! It also has a ton of space and space ship stuff which James Tichenor will tell you he dreads more than anything — unless you ask him about walking, talking Asgard." Confirmation of the challenge 'Exodus' presented to his team is given by the aforementioned visual effects supervisor who nevertheless is proud to announce, "It was pretty hard, but the results were the closest we've come to creating a really great space episode."

"Anyway," continues the executive producer, "Teal'c gets shot and is presumed dead. We always like to tease everyone, including the actors, as to who will be coming back the following season. Except Richard Dean Anderson, of course. It's hard to tease a guy whose name is above the title of the show." Cooper reveals, "The story behind this one will sound familiar. The cost of building the giant space ship set was too prohibitive for just one episode. So, we planned to arc the ship through 'Double Jeopardy', 'Exodus' and then 'Enemies' at the start of season five. In fact, add some fiery sconces and some wacky lighting and the same set doubled as Apophis's ship as well. Hey, you've seen one Peltac..!"

Full of praise for the writers he says, "I know Joe and Paul wrangled with this script a bit, because the timing within the story was a bit tricky. How long does it take for a star to implode after you launch an open gate connected to a black hole into it? Need I say more? We also felt the need to service the Tanith storyline. We had built up this great rivalry between Tanith and Teal'c and then just dropped it for a long time. It's Teal'c's desire to make sure Tanith doesn't escape alive that drags O'Neill into trouble and ultimately gets Teal'c shot in the ambush." Is Teal'c really dead? And will the rest of SG-1 survive? Those season-ending cliffhangers just keep getting bigger… ʎ

Colonel Jack O'Neill

"Looks like you've got yourself a bit of a handful there, George."

As anyone from an airforce chief of staff to an Asgard will testify, Colonel Jack O'Neill is a force to be reckoned with. Not just because of his natural ability in combat in the field, but also his sharp wit, which lies in wait to ambush any unsuspecting victim. In 'Into the Fire' when the vengeful Hathor waves a voracious symbiote in his face in an attempt to invoke some fear, O'Neill quips, "What? The grey doesn't bother you?" No wonder the poor old Queen stormed off in a huff. "I like to incorporate the mischievous elements of my personality with those of Jack O'Neill," confesses Richard Dean Anderson. "It was one of the things I insisted be allowed to happen before I signed on for this job, and I continue to try to get away with as much as I possibly can." Ask any of the other members of the cast and crew and everyone will come up with a shining example of his irreverent approach to life and *Stargate SG-1*. "We do have to put up with a lot of Homer Simpson-isms from Rick," sighs Amanda Tapping. "If any of us fluffs a line or the director suggests some minor change Rick will automatically go 'D'oh!' He makes me smile every time he does it."

Anderson injects more than just his sense of humour into his portrayal of Colonel O'Neill. Some of the practical skills he's learnt along life's path have come in handy every now and then. 'Window of Opportunity' gave him the chance to show off his talent for juggling, a skill learnt out of necessity, as it was the only way that, as a struggling young actor, he could earn enough to buy food other than fruit. "I learned how to juggle when I moved to California, had no money whatsoever and was living in a shack in the backyard of some people's house," he grins. "They had orange, grapefruit and fig trees. Figs were the hardest to juggle because if they got too ripe things got a little messy." Anderson recalls those warm if somewhat sticky days with affection and states, "I have a dear friend named Michael McNeilly. He and I went to college together and we hooked up again out in California. He is the premier clown of all humanity — an extremely funny and talented man. He and I used to work the streets juggling and doing mime and skits and stuff for nickels and dimes. We did whatever it took, but it was kind of imperative I learned to juggle to

that we could draw the crowd." Never serious for very long, Anderson sighs, "Mostly, though, I learned because I had all those oranges, grapefruits and figs to practice with, so not only did I learn to juggle over the course of a summer but I also had a *lot* of vitamin C."

Famously bad at recalling incidents from the filming of specific episodes of *Stargate SG-1*, Anderson is happier to offer his personal opinion or take on a particular story slant: "In 'A Hundred Days', for example, I don't think O'Neill would ever have left Laira if he knew she was pregnant. In fact, if we ever did revisit that story and it turns out O'Neill did father a child, then I'd like to see him with a daughter. That preference is for no reason other than that he's already had a son, and it would be interesting to see how his relationship with a daughter would unfold."

Anderson's relationship with his own daughter would no doubt provide some useful insights. Totally devoted to three year-old Wylie Rose, Anderson says, "There isn't any experience I have with my child that doesn't make me smile. She's my living angel. Her entire personality is just blossoming, exploding out. There are so many tiny things that she does that are innately funny and at times, she'll catch me laughing and she'll ask, 'What's so funny?' and I just have to tell her that what she's doing is absolutely precious and makes me smile." Sharing one such moment he says, "I'm trying to encourage her to learn to swim, so I make sure she wears little water wings and her wetsuit so that she's very, very buoyant, which is important at her age because she would sink like a rock if she weren't! She sees me jump off the side of the pool and, of course, she wants to jump as well, but hasn't quite got the 'blowing out when you go under water' thing — so she gets a mouthful every now and then. She comes up laughing because of the fun factor, but that makes her take in *more* water which makes her choke for a bit, and then she'll start laughing all over again. It's those kinds of moments that I cherish. I love being a dad more than anything."

When he's not doing fun things with his best girl, Anderson can be found throwing himself into various other activities, all of which require loads of energy, stamina and enthusiasm. "I ride bicycles, I run rivers, I climb mountains, but mostly I ski. I live by the ocean so I spend a lot of time in there. Really, I spend most of my time when I'm not with my daughter hanging out in forests and mountains, oceans and rivers."

Anderson's affinity for water is more than just a personal pleasure. Committed to raising awareness of the plight of the peoples who live on or close to some of the world's endangered rivers, he recently returned from a trip down the Upper Yangtze in Tibet, where he filmed an episode of *National Geographic Explorer*. "The experience of running that river was eventful in so many ways," he says, "but during a visit to the last monastery we climbed up to, I was allowed to sit in on a prayer session with all of the monks. One of them grabbed my hand and sat me right down in the middle of one of the rows of chanting monks, and that particular experience was incredibly special to me. Not so much because it was a sacred place to be, and that we had been allowed to film there for our documentary, but because out of nowhere I was led by my hand to be a part of it. It was an all-encompassing experience and I'm not sure I have the words to describe how deeply it touched me."

When he does get the chance to be contemplative nearer to home, Anderson chills by listening to music or reading. Cast away on a remote planet or marooned on a desert island, he has no doubt which artistic material he would take to while away the hours: "My favourite author is Garrison Keillor for a multitude of reasons, not the least of which is he's probably the most insightful, keenest observer of the human race. His *Prairie Home Companion* is just one example where he speaks of, and from, the point of view of a Minnesotan — which is a unique being in the universe. I spend a lot of time listening to his tapes, because he's a wonderful monologist and a great storyteller. Being from Minnesota myself, I get what he says and it makes me laugh. So, I would have to take some of his work with me."

Forced to commit to just three pieces, Anderson is equally definite about the music he would choose to soothe his soul. "The 'Appalachia Waltz' played by Yo-Yo Ma and the 'Prelude to Suite No. 1' from Bach's Unaccompanied Cello Suites. The latter is probably my favourite piece of all time. It's meditative. Oh, and virtually anything by the guitarist and poet Leo Kottke." Reflective, soulful and irreverent in turn — rather like Mr Anderson himself. ⋏

Dr Daniel Jackson

"Major, next time Daniel gets the urge to help someone, shoot him."

Michael Shanks is the first to admit he's made the break from actor James Spader's original interpretation of archaeologist Daniel Jackson in the *Stargate* movie, and has developed the character very much in his own mould. It took a while, though. "I initially decided to stick with James Spader's portrayal first and foremost because it worked well," he explains. "The other consideration was the perception that viewers don't like too many changes all at once when it comes to favourite characters. So I went along with the wisdom at the time, which was to stick close to how the original character was played." Four years down the line, Shanks is delighted that Daniel Jackson has come into his own. "When I look at what we did in seasons one and two of the show, it's hard to believe we are the same group of people. It's amazing to see how far we've come in a relatively short time."

Speaking of the changes he's wrought, Shanks says, "Although Daniel is still very passionate about what he does and how he goes about things, he's grown up a lot in the past two years particularly. When Sha're was first taken, his all-consuming desire was to find her and get her back. In season three, the events in 'Forever in a Day' take that possibility away, and whilst it's a tragedy of sorts, the introduction of the Harsesis child gives Daniel a whole new purpose."

Charged with finding and protecting Sha're's son, Shanks suggests this mission gives him the chance to explore the bittersweet nature of the task. "Daniel has to face up to the challenge of keeping a promise to someone he loved very much, whilst having to swallow the fact that the child was sired by the one person he hates most in the universe. Fortunately, 'Maternal Instinct' gave Daniel the opportunity to let go of that hate and keep his promise. It was quite a turning point for him."

Shanks laughs that the whole Zen Buddhist thing didn't really work for him on a personal level, so 'Maternal Instinct' was an acting challenge in more ways than one. "My mind is less open to that sort of thing than Daniel's so I found it very difficult to get into the mindset. I'm actually more like Jack O'Neill as far as that kind of spiritual journeying is concerned. I have a very cynical point of view about that

type of path. Fortunately, I'm paid to make it look convincing!"

The similarity between Michael Shanks and Jack O'Neill naturally seeps into the relationship between Shanks and Richard Dean Anderson. "I love the banter that's developed between my character and Rick's," Shanks beams. "Towards the middle of season one we discovered that we had the same irreverent sense of humour, and the writers began writing little snippets to let us play with that. Some of the fans have felt that this intimated some sort of rift between us, but it's not like that at all. It's an opportunity for us to have fun, and show there's a deeper understanding between us than is totally evident on the surface."

Empathy aside, O'Neill did try to bump Daniel off in 'Absolute Power'. "Oh yeah! But that was a hoot to do," beams Shanks. "When the producers came to me and asked how I felt about Daniel being perceived as the bad guy for a change I jumped at the chance. It was a wonderful opportunity to show how the Daniel we see every week could behave given a different set of circumstances." As for thwarting O'Neill's attempt to put an end to his shenanigans in that episode, Shanks laughs, "Rick got his own back when I was directing 'Double Jeopardy'. All the other actors were completely up for anything. They knew I was an actor's director and they understood that's what I cared about the most, but Rick is the kind of actor who doesn't take direction — period. I think he only did with me, a bit, to humour me. But I have to say that, basically, he was a pain in the micdah!"

Still smiling, Shanks concedes, "Actually, it was quite an eye-opener for me, because *I'm* usually the one who's trying not to do what the director tells me to do. It was pretty funny having the boot on the other foot." Director Martin Wood insists Shanks is not as bad as he thinks he is: "A couple of times he'd dig his heels in over the way I wanted a particular scene to play, but each time I'd go up and explain, 'This is why I need this to happen this way', and he'd find a way to do it. The whole cast are very good that way."

As well as progressing on the director front, seasons three and four also saw Shanks explore his bent toward writing. "Lots of people give me articles and books and the like because they think that, because I play the character, I personally am interested in archaeology. I occasionally get inundated and can't read them all, but one of our crewmembers gave me a book full of mysteries of South America. I became fascinated with the myth of the crystal skulls and the inconsistencies that surrounded their origin and manufacture. One of the wonderful things about *Stargate* is if we see things like that, we can point to the stars to explain things that happened in the past, so I started to write a story about the skulls." Shanks admits that by the time Michael Greenburg and Jarrad Paul's ideas had been blended with his, and then Brad Wright had polished the whole thing into a producible script, the resulting episode 'Crystal Skull' wasn't quite as they'd expected.

Nevertheless, Shanks is delighted to have been able to follow that particular path. "From an actor's point of view, that episode had the first and only all-green screen set we've ever done, and was a very interesting process. It was funny because you couldn't move a lot. It was too expensive to have us move because it was incredibly difficult visual effects-wise to shift the background away from us to get the right depth and perspective, so we spent a lot of the time locked down. Not an easy thing to do given our natures and personalities!"

Revealing the inquisitive side of his nature, Shanks enthuses, "I'm always fascinated when we get to the end of an episode like 'Crystal Skull' and unleash mysteries that we still can't fathom. It's like *Raiders of the Lost Ark* — just when you think you've solved something, a greater mystery emerges that is beyond our comprehension. I think it's always intriguing when the answer to one thing raises questions which make you continue to explore."

Very happy with the way his role progressed in season four Shanks concludes, "The stories focussed more on Daniel as a person, which is something I always wanted to happen. My hope for the future is that we get to explore his relationships with the other characters in more depth, and get to find out more about what makes Daniel tick." Å

"I have great confidence in you, Carter. Go back to the SGC and confuse Hammond."

The phrase 'never a dull moment' could have been coined for both actress Amanda Tapping and the character she portrays, Major Samantha Carter. "Let's see," muses Tapping, "I've been infected by a Goa'uld; unofficially adopted a child; had the odd dalliance with a couple of aliens; admitted my feelings for Jack O'Neill; got married; died. Oh — and I got to be superwoman." Not bad for the gal who started out as the lone female fighting her way into 'the biggest boys club in the world.'

"I'm actually very happy with where Sam is now, although there is still some way to go with regard to developing her relationships with Teal'c and Daniel. But on the whole I'm pleased with how things have progressed over the past couple of years. I am much happier with the character now." Acknowledging that, "Right from the start, Sam has always been the one with the facts and figures at her disposal," Tapping explains, "she can say all that technical jargon without missing a beat, and whilst almost all of it is absolutely necessary for the exposition of the story, for an actor, it can get kind of boring."

Determined not to let the character become too tedious, Tapping says, "One of the things I've tried to do throughout the series is look for the interesting moments in scenes and play with them. Even something as simple as a slight facial movement can convey a part of the story. I owe it to myself as much as to the audience to flex my 'acting muscles' as much as possible, so that I'm constantly communicating little bits of Sam into the mix."

Director Martin Wood thinks Tapping is a master at the art. "Amanda is a director's delight," he smiles. "Without a doubt she is absolutely the easiest of the entire cast to work with, because she will always do whatever you ask. If you ask her to do something she will always find her own reason for it. She is also the easiest to cut to, because she's always got expression on her face. Even if the main focus is on another actor, Amanda is always acting and all the directors love her for that. She's so dependable."

Whilst Tapping agrees 'dependable' is good, one of the things she enjoys most about working on *SG-1* is that nothing is ever quite that predictable. At a time when so many of the sci-fi shows on television

dance round the prospect of a romance between the main male and female characters, *Stargate* has gone against the grain and knocked the idea of a sexual liaison between Carter and O'Neill firmly on the head.

Speaking of the resolution of the 'do they/don't they love each other' debate, Tapping emphatically supports the writers' decision to 'clear the air'. "Sam and Jack were never meant to be together. Not just from a military point of view, but for all sorts of reasons. He would drive her crazy for starters! I love the way the writers brought the situation to the fore in 'Divide and Conquer' and had the courage to let them admit their love for each other, acknowledge that it was never to be and then let them get on with the rest of their lives." Adding her own insouciant touch she smirks, "Sam did have other fish to fry, you know. She does, or did, have other admirers." Laughing that there is obviously some plot afoot to stop Sam Carter from finding true love, she sighs, "It's such a shame they made me bump off Martouf, though. Maybe I could talk the producers into bringing him back…"

Joking aside, the actress is proud to portray a strong female character that doesn't exactly shun male attention, and is perfectly comfortable being a single, well adjusted woman, happy with who she is and where she is in life. "A lot of the single women characters on TV today are frantically searching for Mr Right, and feel their lives are unfulfilled without him. Not Sam! Not that I want her to come across as smug or anything like that, but she can stand back and say, 'You know what? I love and am loved by my family and friends. I'm good at what I do. I like my job and the people I work with. I'm a success.'

"That to me is one of the greatest things about how Sam has developed over the years. She's grown from being the hard-assed, stereotypical 'feminist in the military' type into this strong, positive, happy female. I've had so many fans come up to me to let me know how much

Sam's attitude has influenced their personal lives in a good way. It's extremely humbling to know that something I do on a television show can have that profound an effect. It makes me so proud to be a part of this show, and I pray that the writers will continue to stay on top of things and continue to allow Sam to develop in that same vein."

Fiercely protective of the show and loathe to proffer any negative thoughts about it, Tapping admits she hasn't always been so enamoured with the producers' and writers' tack regarding women on *Stargate SG-1*. Displaying the honesty and openness for which she is famed, Tapping begins, "Let me preface this by saying that Vanessa Angel is a wonderful, smart woman and was tremendous to work alongside. But I am glad the character of Anise went away. One of the things which has always made me proud about our show is that for so many years we've never resorted to overtly sexual tactics to get people to watch *Stargate SG-1*.

"I think — and the fans' reaction seemed to bear this out — that to have some of the best and most interesting story lines in our history compromised by having a woman whose body was so stunning it could stop the traffic parading around in skimpy little outfits, was somehow beneath the high standard we had set for ourselves. Vanessa Angel is a bright, intelligent actor. She would have delivered a great performance whatever they clothed her in. We've had lots of beautiful women on the show, but for different reasons. My feeling is that Anise's tiny costumes were a blatant attempt to make the show sexier. I mean, look at the stories we told in the 'Upgrades'/'Divide and Conquer' arc: O'Neill and Sam finally admit their love for each other, the Tok'ra alliance is strengthened and Martouf dies. There are major things happening in these episodes and I think we sold ourselves short by adding that unnecessary element."

All of that said, Tapping does feel the writers have done Carter proud in the past couple of years: "In 'The Devil You Know', we got to see quite a bit about Carter's family background, and how far the relationship between Carter and her father has come since her mother died. Numerous times we've seen that she is a fully functioning red-blooded woman who is attracted to members of the opposite sex, even if they do end up dead — in every freakin' case I might add! In 'Prodigy' we saw how committed she is to building the future teams of personnel at the SGC. My hope for Sam's future," Tapping concludes, "is that we get some insight into the other relationships she's had as an adult woman." Stay tuned... ⅄

Teal'c

Teal'c

"If I were still loyal to the Goa'uld you would know it. It would be immediately apparent, as I would not hesitate to kill you where you sit."

Until season three, Earth's strong and silent resident alien, Teal'c, could be relied upon to face every challenge presented to SG-1 with calm stoicism and nothing more than a well-timed lift of a brow. How things have changed. Christopher Judge is delighted the Jaffa's true personality has been allowed to come to the fore in the show's middle seasons. "To be honest I was getting a little tired of keeping the stony face," grins Judge, "especially when it's the complete antithesis of my own, shall we say, *ebullient* nature. I mean, four years down the line, it would have appeared strange had Teal'c not started to display some of his latent human attributes. He is from human stock. It stands to reason that, removed from constant exposure to the stronger elements of the Goa'uld, he would revert to type at some time or other, and begin to show the more acceptable side of his make-up." Judge cites the episode 'Learning Curve' as an example of where Teal'c's gentler side is allowed to slip through: "Teal'c is genuinely pleased to have formed a warm relationship with the child, Tomin, is truly concerned for his welfare, and deeply distressed when he is reduced to a vegetative state. Whether or not the warmth Teal'c shows towards the boy stems from the relationship with his own son is a moot point. The fact is, Teal'c likes and is comfortable around children. That's not something you'd expect from a Goa'uld-infested Jaffa!"

Another unexpected development during seasons three and four is Teal'c's burgeoning sense of humour. "It's always been there, you know. He was just waiting for an appropriate time to show it," Judge winks. "I loved 'Point of No Return', because you get to see the lighter side of Teal'c in so many different ways. The 'magic fingers' bed gag was a delight, and I loved the fact that you were never quite sure whether or not Teal'c was being vindictive when he refused to allow Marty his medication, and banished him to the bathroom. I think the producers' timing has been particularly apropos with regard to revealing the character's lighter side."

With an inherent sense of the ridiculous and a predisposition towards wicked behaviour, it's no wonder Judge struggles to keep a straight face during some of the more frivolous episodes of the show. "If

114 STARGATE THE ILLUSTRATED COMPANION

you watch 'Urgo'," he chuckles, "you'll see that there are hardly any shots of Teal'c. That's because there were very few where I'm not doubled over with laughter! Dom DeLuise is a very funny man and to watch his son Peter encouraging his Dad's outrageous behaviour was, in itself, hilarious."

Outstanding guest stars aside, Judge admits that any of his co-stars can reduce him to a helpless state: "Richard Dean Anderson has one of the most wicked senses of humour known to man, and I'm not even going to try to describe how duplicitous and down right sneaky Michael Shanks can be when he wants to!" Judge has never forgiven Shanks for terrifying the life out of him by pretending there was a bear in the woods whilst they were shooting an early episode of the show. "There was some sort of payback in season four though," Judge says, "when a bear actually *did* wander into frame while Shanks was shooting a scene for 'Scorched Earth'. The shoe was definitely on the other foot then! Of course, I had some important business to attend to in my trailer, so had to remove myself from the scene and wasn't around to tease him that much." Nothing to do with being scared of the bear, then.

During the first two seasons of the show, Teal'c was a man of few words, a situation which the actor felt was entirely appropriate for the character at that time: "Teal'c was listening, and observing the ways of the culture he'd been adopted into, and was learning how to get his feelings across in the most appropriate manner. It felt very natural just to let him stand back and watch, and then take little forays into this new environment. One thing I've learned playing this character is that less is more. As an actor you always feel you should be doing something, and as a person I'm never still. I'm always moving around, joking around — doing something. But when you are just standing there observing what is going on around you — people become curious about your thoughts and your motives. So although Teal'c didn't have a lot to say for himself in the first two seasons, he's now choosing to open his mouth, but only when the situation warrants it. He allows his stillness to speak for him."

That said, by seasons three and four Teal'c had definitely learnt how to better express himself verbally. "He's really participating more by offering his input," Judge agrees, "rather than just following O'Neill into battle. In 'Scorched Earth', for instance, O'Neill asks why he didn't try to stop Daniel from going back to the 'enemy' ship, and Teal'c says it's because he didn't entirely disagree with what Daniel was trying to do. It was one of those times where we see that Teal'c does now feel comfortable enough to offer a direct challenge. I think that's because he stopped feeling like an outsider, and really feels like part of the team rather than just the muscle who helps beat up the bad guys when needed. His relationship with everyone in SG-1, and Jack O'Neill in particular, has really warmed up. I *loved* it when we did all the crazy stuff in 'Window of Opportunity', like the golf and the juggling, and supporting each other when we were regurgitating Carter's technobabble or correcting Daniel's linguistic translations. The understated bond between Teal'c and O'Neill was fun to do."

The Jaffa's relationships with members of his own race have been given more attention, too. "It's a development which pleases me greatly," smirks Judge. "In 'Crossroads' we actually see him involved in a relationship with a woman from his past, and the depth of emotion he displays takes everyone by surprise. Not just in that episode, but later on when his determination to get Tanith puts both Teal'c and O'Neill in peril. I'm grateful to the writers for allowing a glimpse of the passion he restrains to slip through. I mean passion in the widest sense, not just the sexual form, you understand. I'd like them to explore that a lot more throughout the next couple of years."

Usually willing to at least think about the actors' hopes and suggestions for the future, one development the producers will not be taking forward is Judge's request for facial hair. Their short brush with Teal'c's blonde "chin tickler", as Peter DeLuise coined the inch-long tuft of hair sported by the Jaffa at the beginning of season four, was quite enough, it seems. "Hey, Teal'c is an independent spirit," Judge reasons, "with a sense of humour and not many opportunities for levity. I thought it could have been incorporated as part of Teal'c's ongoing assimilation process." Whatever else lies in store for the mighty Jaffa, it's safe to say that hair and a beard will not be high on the agenda! ⋏

General Hammond

"There's a man who is very important to me. He's bald and wears a short sleeved shirt. I think his name is Homer."

As the man responsible for keeping the Stargate Command Centre and the errant SG-1 under control, General George Hammond earns every penny of his commission. Not content to be the sort of officer who sits behind a desk blithely issuing orders, Hammond is there, watching, sometimes even standing by the Gate as his teams depart and, he hopes, return safely from their often perilous missions.

"There is a myth that officers in high positions can simply turn off their emotions and order their troops to do whatever it takes, even lay down their lives, in order to get the job done. That doesn't happen in real life," insists actor Don S. Davis. "I come from a military background. I was a captain in the US Army so have some inkling of what it is to be a soldier. Hammond is smart enough to know that when he sends them out and tells them to 'go save the world', his teams will try their best to do just that, but they won't necessarily do it by following his orders to the letter. What I try to bring to the character is a sense of care and compassion for the men and women under his command; trying to let them know that their personal welfare is uppermost in his mind, even when the stakes are high."

Davis is particularly happy to have been given a greater chance to show that side of Hammond's personality throughout seasons three and four: "In 'Crystal Skull', Hammond finally got to express some fondness for Dr Jackson. There's a scene when Hammond has to tell one of his granddaughters — who incidentally are the lights of his life — that he can't attend a school event because he has to try to find a dear friend. Hammond has no idea that Daniel can hear him at the time, but I thought it was a wonderful way of showing the depth of feeling the General has for these people, even if he can't exactly wear his heart on his sleeve or show any kind of favouritism in the normal course of events."

That said, there have been several occasions when Hammond has gone that extra mile, often putting himself on the line for his top team. "'Into the Fire' was one example where Hammond committed a court-martial-able offence to get out there and try to save SG-1," Davis points out. "By leaving the base and stepping through the

Stargate, he was directly defying his own standing orders, but he knew it was the right thing to do. One of the things I like most about Hammond is that whilst he's a by-the-book sort of man, he will think for himself and act accordingly." Davis says this is also apparent in the season four story 'Chain Reaction', when the character resigns rather than be a figurehead for some shady government agency. "Hammond is nobody's fool. He's a man of honour and will do whatever it takes to maintain that integrity."

Whilst Davis professes that being a part of *Stargate SG-1* is in itself a reward, the actor was doubly thrilled to be invited to join the personnel in the high security base in the real life Cheyenne Mountain, in Colorado. "General Michael Ryan from the Air Force was invited to guest star in 'Prodigy' and in return he invited me to be his guest at the Air Force versus Navy football game. Then General Eberhart, the head of NORAD, arranged a tour of the high security facility. It was an amazing experience for me and truly one of the highlights of my career. I was even invited to address the Air Force Academy, which was quite a feat, given that I didn't have the benefit of Brad Wright or Robert Cooper writing the script!"

Away from the rigours of Stargate Command, Don Davis is one of those people who needs to be working to stay out of mischief. Blessed with insatiable curiosity and a wicked sense of humour, he claims, "I like to keep busy, and don't know what to do with myself if I'm not working on *Stargate SG-1*. In fact, it's imperative that I stay focussed on some project, otherwise I'd just get into trouble!" Not that he has that much spare time on his hands. During the breaks from filming Davis appeared in several national and international films, all of which have been well received.

"I've made a couple of independent movies," he says. "I was with Michael Shanks in *Suspicious River* and *The Artists Circle*, plus I teamed up with Teryl Rothery in the comedy *Best in Show*." This hilarious, mostly improvised film, about a prestigious dog show, had Davis honing his hitherto undiscovered talent as a top judge. "I had to learn all sorts of things, particularly how to examine a dog from head to foot and, ah, all the parts in between. All I can tell you is how grateful I am that all the dogs I had to touch were incredibly well behaved."

As if the lure of film studios weren't enough, Davis also tries to find the time to work in his art studio. "I have a life-long passion for the visual arts and love to paint, sculpt and draw. At the moment I've just completed several pieces which I intend to sell on the Internet." Davis's first love is abstract, but in order to give people a feel for who he is as an artist, his current collection comprises an eclectic group of pieces that includes nudes, landscapes, portraits and still life works.

The actor's recent trip to the UK to attend the SG-3 fan convention meant that Davis was close enough to mainland Europe to pay a visit to France. "I met up with a friend in Paris who took me to some of the best private galleries in the city." He chuckles, "With absolutely no shame at all, he told the owners that I was a very important person from the United States and they opened the doors for me. I was like a kid in a candy store and had a wonderful, wonderful time. Seeing the variety and talent that abounds there was truly inspiring."

Davis may have found the inspiration to continue his art works but what are his thoughts on the future for General Hammond? "Well, I keep hoping against hope that the writers will think of some way to show Hammond as a man of passion. With the exception of Dr Fraiser, everyone else has been in some kind of romantic relationship. Sometimes more than one. I think it's high time Hammond stopped fondling his medals and got out more!"

Just in case the powers that be need a nudge in the right direction, Davis has his eye on the woman he'd most like to see snuggled up with Hammond. Eyes twinkling he smiles, "I have the greatest admiration for Xenia Seeberg who plays Xev in the sci-fi show *Lexx*. Apart from her obvious attributes, I've heard she's a charming young lady. Maybe I should pull rank to get her on our show." It remains to be seen whether the producers of *Stargate SG-1* take the wishes of their commanding officer into account... λ

Dr Janet Fraiser

"Dr Fraiser believes you are not strong enough to undertake such a mission."

"Yeah, whatever... " [thud].

Stand by your beds. Dr Fraiser is in the house. When Teryl Rothery first took up the challenge of portraying the young medical officer at the SGC, she was given to understand that the part "may recur". Four years down the line, Janet Fraiser has become part and parcel of Stargate Command's team, the medical lynchpin that keeps the troops battle ready and fighting fit. "Not that they always pay attention to her advice," says Rothery with a wry grin. "Most of the SG teams share the same gung ho attitude but, as the heroes of the show, SG-1 in particular almost always ignore any threat to themselves in order to get the job done. They tend to look at things from an immediate security standpoint, rather than take the medical or scientific concerns into consideration. It's Janet's job to make them see sense."

As feisty as she is focussed, Fraiser can certainly fulfil that part of the challenge with aplomb. Faced with O'Neill's constant whining about lights being shone in his eyes during 'Window of Opportunity', Fraiser's steely glare manages to silence the man faster than a threat from any System Lord. "I love the dynamic between Janet and O'Neill," Rothery smiles. "It's one born out of mutual respect and genuine affection, although the fear of a jab in the nether regions or an extra day's confinement in the sick bay does help to keep him in line." Neat, petite and very discreet, Dr Fraiser would never voluntarily give away any secrets unless the lives of her SG patients depended upon it. As Rothery puts it, "A teeny example is when she tries to get Sam to take a break from finding a way to rescue Jack in 'A Hundred Days'. Janet is well aware of the feelings Sam has for O'Neill, but wouldn't dream of discussing them unless Sam opened the conversation."

Rothery is very pleased with the way her character has been allowed to develop over the past couple of years. "In seasons three and four we really get to reveal some of the facets that make Janet what she is, and get to see how some of the relationships have been nurtured and developed. One of my favourite episodes is 'Legacy', where SG-1 and I are infected by some alien technology unwittingly carried back to Earth by Daniel. We got to see a very different side of Fraiser then. I loved that we got to see Janet gradually lose control of her body and mind, and that she still fought so hard

to find a cure. Usually she is the calm and collected one who keeps everything together. It was a treat to get to play her in such a vulnerable position."

Rothery also enjoyed playing the bad girl in season three's 'Foothold'. "I was having so much fun with it that our director Andy Mikita had to get me to tone it down a notch. Talk about over the top productions — Colonel O'Neill actually gets to thump a woman in this one. He turns around and bops 'bad' Fraiser in the face!" Praising Richard Dean Anderson, Rothery states, "A previous neck injury means I have to be very careful making any sharp or sudden moves, but Richard was so great, he positioned me so that when I fell back from his 'punch', I landed in the best possible way to protect my neck and spine." Unfortunately, Mr Anderson wasn't quite so careful when it came to removing the alien cloaking device. "I have no idea what they used to stick that little bugger on my chest, but when Richard ripped it off, my skin came with it! I was bruised for weeks."

After physically fighting with Jack O'Neill, Rothery thoroughly enjoyed pitting Fraiser's wit against that of the Tok'ra Anise. "In 'Upgrades', Anise experiments on SG-1 with the armbands that are believed to bring amazing strength to help beat the Goa'uld, but which are actually harmful to the carriers. I particularly liked this episode because we get to see how much Janet will fight for those she loves. She has come to feel a great deal about the people she now sees as family. In 'Upgrades' and the later 'Divide and Conquer' you get to see Janet the friend, the co-worker and protective doctor to SG-1. She does not like Anise *at all* in these episodes, and it shows. That in itself was a challenge, because Vanessa Angel was lovely to work with. We had a really great time."

Another favourite was season four's 'Entity': "Sam gets taken over by an alien artificial intelligence and it was a great episode to showcase Janet's strength as a doctor, as well as allowing her emotions to show regarding her love for Sam as her friend. It was a very touching episode. One that I am very proud of."

Whilst Dr Fraiser can wield considerable medical expertise to help keep the SGC on its feet, Teryl Rothery on the other hand is prone to over-zealous fits of emotional behaviour for which there is no known cure. The occurrence is completely unpredictable, and only Rothery herself can really describe this strange condition...

Lady Rothery's Fan
By Teryl Rothery

I'm afraid that on occasion, I'm known for bursting into fits of hysterical laughter on set. A prime example was when we were filming '2010'. There is a moment where Daniel, Teal'c, Sam and her husband Joe and I are standing around at their award ceremony, drinking champagne and toasting the late General Hammond (don't forget, we are meant to be ten years into the future). Anyway, in this scene, an Aschen character called Mollem makes his entrance and I/Janet am supposed to acknowledge him with a greeting. We shot the master take, and then it was time for a two-shot of Shanks and myself. Now this is all a bit technical, but our eye-line to Mollem had changed, so that when the actor entered we weren't supposed to look at him. We were meant to look at a piece of tape attached to the side of the camera. Well, when we were filming, the actor entered, only I forgot to 'cheat' and looked straight at him. Instead of letting it go and carrying on, I came out of character and stammered, 'Oh... I... Oops!' It could all have worked out, because throughout all of this everyone else ignored my goof and kept acting the scene. That would have been great, except I got the giggles and couldn't bring myself under control. I looked up at Michael Shanks and laughed. Rather helpfully, he reacted to this by making a bunch of funny faces, which made me laugh even more. Then I just totally lost it. Tears were rolling down my face. I was doubled over and worse than that, I was *snorting*! Yes, Teryl Rothery *snorts* when she loses control. When poor Andy Mikita, our director, finally called 'Cut!', I was a complete mess. Fortunately, help was at hand to get the episode finished on time, but the make-up department had their work cut out to get me back together again. I remember Jan Newman, our make-up supervisor yelling, 'Where's Teryl's fan? Get her fan!' You see, I am so well known for this hysteria, and, I might add, for bursting into tears at the drop of a hat if someone tells me a sad story, that the make-up department actually keeps a fan in my make-up bag, so they can 'fan dry' my eyes. Forget *anything* about me being cool, calm and collected. That only happens in the *Stargate* universe! Λ

Recurring Characters

Brad Wright

"We pride ourselves on having an interesting, eclectic group of characters, that we can revisit time and again."

Over the years, *Stargate SG-1* has built up a rich and varied roster of recurring characters, from evil Goa'uld System Lords and duplicitous officers of the US military, to the benevolent Asgard and peace-loving Tok'ra. Too many characters, alas, to cover in detail, but here are three of the most familiar faces…

"I had just finished a movie called *The Inspectors* and was brought in to read for the part of a bad Tok'ra," recalls actor JR Bourne. "In the audition room Brad Wright asked if I would read for the **Martouf** character, then said, 'Can you do it nicer?' Richard Dean Anderson heard me and said, 'I think he'd be great.' Oh happy day!"

Martouf and Sam Carter hit it off straight away. It may have something to do with the fact that he was the partner of the symbiote that inhabited the lady's body for a short time, but Amanda Tapping maintains, "It looked as though he was the only chance Sam had for some loving. I can't believe they made me kill him!" The character's dramatic demise in 'Divide and Conquer' came as a real shock to fans. "I can only hope that the adage that 'nobody dies in science fiction' holds true for Martouf," Tapping sighs.

Possessed of the most sparkling blue eyes, with a personality and acting talent to match, the lovely Martouf swiftly sailed into the hearts of Gatewatchers everywhere, many of whom share Ms Tapping's hopes for the gallant Tok'ra's future. Across the Internet, campaigns have sprung up insisting 'Martouf Lives', whilst the producers are being constantly bombarded with pleas of "Bring Back Martouf".

As for the man himself, Bourne has been off filming a movie, called *Cabin by the Lake*. However, hope is at hand. "I may just pop up in *Stargate*'s season five," he reveals. "Watch this space…"

Opposite page and above: Martouf off-duty — JR Bourne at Gatecon.

Sergeant Siler's Story
By Dan Shea

Sergeant First Class Sylvester Siler II, 'Sly' to his friends, was born in Cincinnati in the swingin' sixties and moved to Syracuse when he was sixteen. He graduated from Syracuse University majoring in all the sciences. His hobbies are soccer, surfing, snowboarding, synchronised swimming, sailing and skiing at Whistler (an obsession for which he leases a Silverado). His favourite cinema films are *Return of the Secaucus Seven*, *Sixteen Candles*, *Sliver*, *Sweet Sixteen*, *The Great Escape* and all Steven Segal movies. His favourite drinks are Slurpees, Schlitz and Singapore Slings. His favourite foods are sushi, seafood, spaghetti and souvlaki. He wears Serengeti sunglasses and rides his Schwinn or drives his Saab to show off. Sergeant Siler was assigned to the Stargate in '97, where he is an expert in wormholes and Stellular Interface elements.

Sergeant Siler may be silly with his sibilant sounds but in real life Dan Shea, who is also the stunt co-ordinator, and the man responsible for safety on set, has more trouble with his little finger than anything else: "I double for Richard Dean Anderson and love all the action stuff, but I do have one problem. I can't seem to hold my pinky in when I'm firing a gun! So I'll come in in the morning, say 'Hi' and Rick will hold up his little finger to let me know I've messed up again." Oh, sh — sugar! There's one thing that Siler is never without, as Shea explains: "Usually, whenever you see me walking by, I'm holding a wrench. It started off as just a normal wrench, but over the years they kept giving me bigger and bigger ones, and the one I carry around now is the same size as I am! I guess it must be for cranking up the Stargate," he jokes.

Above: Sgt Siler Slurping Sprite — Dan Shea at Gatecon.

Whilst his character **Sergeant Davis**, the 'Technician', may dream of jumping through the Stargate to visit other planets, actor Gary Jones knows there'll be a welcome in the hillside should he ever return home to his native Wales: "I left there when I was about eight and can actually remember all my aunties and neighbours and friends waving us off from the railway station to this unknown universe. Our departure to the ends of the known world was even reported in the daily newspaper!"

Fortunately, Jones didn't vanish off the face of the Earth, but resurfaced in Canada, did all the usual growing up things, and ended up as the 'Technician' on *Stargate SG-1*. "When I first joined the show, I was very much just an extra cast member. But over the years I've progressed to having a name and even a rank — Sergeant Davis. Good eh?"

A stand-up comedian as well as an actor who treads the boards, Jones can boast several theatrical roles in addition to almost thirty roles in film and television, including *World's Greatest Guy, Homeward Bound, Sliders* and *Highlander*. All of which stands him in good stead when it comes to portraying the guy who has initiated the Stargate cycle more times than anybody else. "There's a great buzz on that set," he says.

*Above: Sgt Davis —
'Gate Traffic
Controller.*

"You never know quite what you're in for when you turn up for *Stargate* and for me, that's what makes it such a great gig." Just how Jones got that gig is a story that's best left to the man himself...

Learning to Love Chevrons
By Gary Jones

Five years ago I auditioned for *Stargate SG-1*. My agent at the time told me that there was a 'slight chance' of it becoming a recurring role. So, she felt that I should go in there and be extra great to make them want me back. "*Extra* great?" I said. "What do you mean by that?" She said, "You know, be on time, be more than accommodating and don't let anything be a problem." "Well," I said, "I'm like that *anyway*." She replied, "Whatever. Just don't screw yourself out of a potential long-term job."

The pilot episode was being directed by a huge man named Mario Azzopardi. I walk into the audition and, recognising me from a previous *Outer Limits* episode that he'd directed me in, he practically hugs and kisses me, yelling, "It's *you*! It's *you*! You're *perfect* for this role!" Try to imagine what this does to an actor's self-esteem when a director says this

Above: Chevrons are a serious business.

to them in an audition. In my head I'm thinking, "Well, you might as well tell the other losers auditioning for this to go home."

Mario has… well, the term 'massive energy' doesn't quite do it justice, but you get the picture. The guy's from Malta so he's got the accent thing going for him, coupled with the fact that he's as high-strung as a race horse on laxatives. When he loves you, you're untouchable. When he hates you, death can't come quick enough. In the audition, he loves me. Mario goes into this long, mangled explanation of what my character, the 'Technician' is all about. About two sentences in, I zone out because, well, who cares? I don't really need to listen because I got the part, right? Suddenly, Mario makes reference to some other character in some other film in which he sees similarities to *my* 'Technician'. I give him a cursory nod and an "Uh-huh" and basically wait for Mario to flit to some other subject. But hold on! He's still talking about this *other character* that I've paid zero attention to. What the hell is he talking about in that garbled accent? And I realise in that moment that I have to come clean with Mario. I have to tell him that I haven't seen the film he's talking about, and I don't know that character he's referring to. But hey, what harm can come of that? I've got the part anyway. Right? And this loud giant *loves* me. So I interrupt him and say, very off-handedly, "Uh, Mario, I haven't seen that film and I have no idea who that character is." Mario's diatribe sputters to and end and he just stares at me.

Uh-oh.

Those of you who saw the film *The Perfect Storm* will understand the idea of various sources of negative energy converging into one place, creating a force of nature that flattens everything in its path. In Mario's case, all the pockets of negativity and brooding swirling around in various parts of his person all headed for his face, to create what I like to call *The Perfect Frown*. His face became so blood-engorged and dark that I had to take a step back. "You haven't seen it? You haven't seen the film I'm talking about? You don't know this character?" he growls. "Uh, no," I say. "Then why the *hell* are you standing there nodding your head? WHY AM I WASTING MY TIME TALKING ABOUT THIS?!!" "Because... because... because I liked hearing you talk," I say. Mario stares at me and he bursts out laughing. "Right, right. Okay, let's read this script."

So I sit down with my audition pages. I sit in front of the imaginary console that I've now sat at for five years. The lines that I have to read are these: "Incoming traveller! Incoming traveller!" General Hammond tells me to open the Stargate and then I say: "Chevron One, encoded. Chevron Two, encoded. Chevron Three, encoded. Chevron Four, encoded. Chevron Five, encoded. Chevron Six, encoded. Chevron Seven... *locked*." It was like reading a grocery list. As an actor, you're told to go into an audition with *something*. Something to make your reading interesting and memorable. What the hell do you do when you're simply encoding seven chevrons? And plus, what the hell's a chevron?

I just did what I had been trained to do. I made it funny. I started off normally but by the time I got to the seventh chevron, I was doing Jerry Lewis, yelling, 'Hey, *LADY!!!!!*' Brad Wright and Michael Greenburg, the executive producers, were banging the table laughing. And Mario! My God, could the guy laugh any louder? It totally egged me on so that by the end of the audition, I wasn't so much acting as I was *busking*. All the while thinking, "This is in the bag." So I finish and look around, and I'm kind of hoping that they'll tell me right there and then that I got the job, but of course, they didn't because they never do. Mario's wiping tears of laughter from his eyes. He goes, 'That was great. That was great.' And I swagger to the door, knowing that I have the part. And as I swing open the door and take a step out, Mario adds, 'But, really, it should be nowhere near that big, right?' And I laugh and say, 'Right!' And then I close the door and stand there wanting to shoot myself in the head because now I know that I blew it! I was too big!! They let me hang myself!!!

I spent the next couple of days doing a lot of stretching, so that I could eventually kick myself in the ass. I also went over and over the audition trying to figure out where it all went wrong. Kind of like what you do after you've been in a car wreck and you obsess, trying to figure out what you could've done to avoid it. Which is nothing, because you never saw the other car coming anyway — much like I never saw behind the laughter of the audition that I was trying to get a job on a serious sci-fi show.

But you know what? I *did* get the job and thankfully, for the last five years, Chevron Seven has, indeed, been locked! ⅄

Production Design

Paul Mullie

"I'm amazed that I can visualise a scene in my head when I'm writing it, and Richard and his team deliver more or less the exact same thing."

Whenever you see SG-1 running around a grubby medieval village, or wandering about a shiny space ship, spare a thought for the hard-working group of talented individuals who design, build and maintain those glorious sets. According to award-winning production designer Richard Hudolin, the team slogan is "Scripts? We don't need no stinkin' scripts!" coined because work on the complicated structures is always well underway before a single line of dialogue is committed to paper. "You must understand that when we begin the process of designing a set, we don't have anything as formal as a script," he explains. "How it starts is we'll be talking with [executive producers] Robert Cooper or Brad Wright, and, taking the episode 'The Curse' as an example, they'll say something like 'We've got to go into a tomb!' My colleague Doug McLean and I will ask, 'Well, what sort of tomb? How many rooms? How many hallways? What happens in this tomb?' At that point they'll usually admit that they haven't exactly *written* anything yet, but they'd like some special little touches — a sarcophagus here, a sliding wall there. Nothing too challenging, you understand!

"The challenge comes from trying to re-visit existing sets and materials without our audience realising we're doing it," Hudolin continues. "The nature of *Stargate* is that we're constantly trying to produce movie-quality sets on a television budget, so anything we can recycle is used to the max." Whilst it may seem that such a frugal attitude toward film production is laudable, Hudolin yells, "Are you kidding? You'd tear your hair out trying to figure out how to use some of this stuff again and again. Doug and I often just scratch our heads and think, 'What the hell are we going to do with this now? This is its third use!'" A typical example is the cargo ship built for 'Deadman's Switch'. "We were only supposed to use that thing once," confides Doug McLean, "but we ended up using it about fourteen times."

One of the biggest tests to the production team's ingenuity was the main set for 'Jolinar's Memories'/'The Devil You Know'. "It was supposed to be a representation of Hell," grins Hudolin, "but I just call it Hell." Colleague McLean claims, "It wasn't that bad. Certainly it was one of our biggest ventures. It took over sound stage six — which in itself

Opposite page:
Concept drawings for Osiris's ship in 'The Curse'.
Page 134:
Production design for the Isis Jar in 'The Curse' (top) and the bounty hunter's ship in 'Deadman's Switch' (bottom).

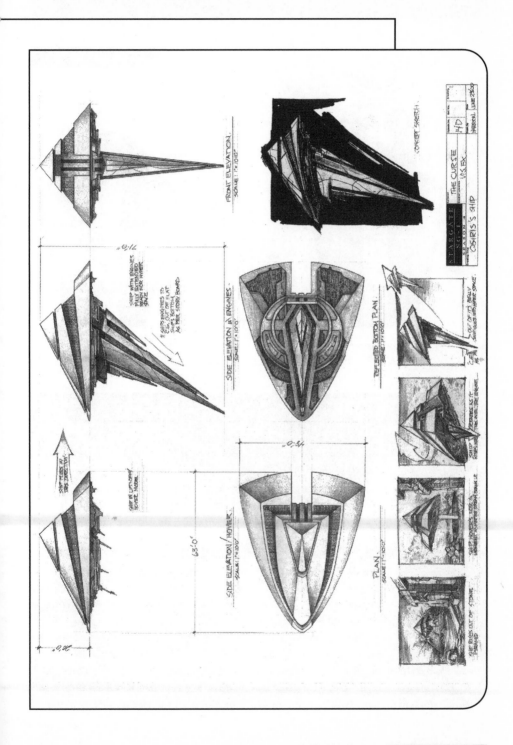

FRONT ELEVATION.
SCALE: 1" = 10'-0"

CONCEPT SKETCH.

STARGATE
SG-1
SEASON 6
THE CURSE
V5 EX.
OSIRIS'S SHIP

SIDE ELEVATION IN ENGINES.
SCALE: 1" = 10'-0"

REFLECTED BOTTOM PLAN.
SCALE: 1" = 10'-0"

SIDE ELEVATION / HOVER.
SCALE: 1" = 10'-0"

PLAN.
SCALE: 1" = 10'-0"

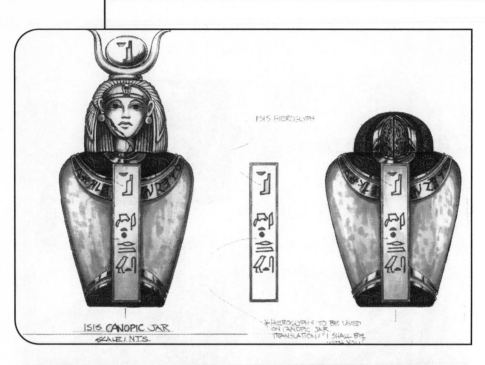

ISIS HIEROGLYPH

ISIS CANOPIC JAR
SCALE: N.T.S.

*HIEROGLYPHS TO BE USED
ON CANOPIC JAR
TRANSLATION: "I SHALL BE
WITH YOU"

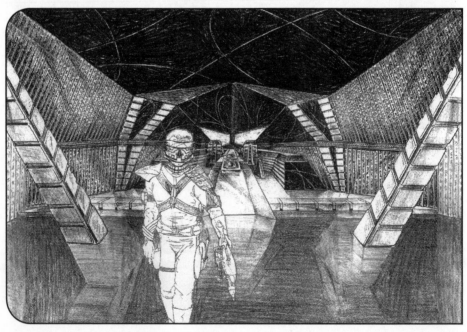

Page 135:
Production drawing
of Hell, from 'Jolinar's
Memories'/'The Devil
You Know'.
Above: *Design for*
the indoor village set
in 'Demons'.

is massive — and we would have built more but we ran out of space and money! It was a lot of fun though, because we wound up re-using lots of bits from old shows. Much of the texture on the walls came out of the mud huts we built for a previous episode, 'One False Step'. They were whitewashed domes on the outside, but foam on the inside, and we'd kept them for ages trying to figure out a use for them. We couldn't just throw them out. We ended up breaking them apart, flattening them out and using the inside as the basis for the textural structure of Hell."

Expanding on the idea that the two-part episode wasn't as difficult to design as Hudolin makes out, McLean adds, "In a funny way, that set almost designed itself. There was actually a lot of work to make it 'design itself', but it was one of those times when everyone really got into the groove and kept adding their own touches along the way, so that it just kept getting better and better."

Though they were very much *simpatico* from the start, another aspect that keeps improving is the production team's relationship with the show's writers and producers. "You know, we've never started

something and have them come back and tell us it doesn't correspond to what they've written," McLean points out proudly. "In practice, they actually write to what we're designing. They are pretty good that way. Of course, it happens occasionally that in the process — as we're designing — one of them will come down and go, 'Yeah! That's perfect. Great! Now he goes out this door...' and we'll go, 'Door? What door? You didn't mention a door the last time we spoke!' And their response will be, 'Oh yeah! We need doors at both ends, sorry.'" Insisting that no crimes have been committed, Hudolin swears that he and his team are nothing if not patient, and that the full complement of writers and producers is accounted for. "It's the good relationship that saves them a lot of the time, because when we go back to the writers and tell them we can do what they want but it will cost a certain amount, they'll look at our designs and go, 'Wow! This is great. We need to use that set more.' Often they will increase the size of a scene to accommodate what we've created."

Hudolin is particularly proud, though not surprised, that throughout the entire time he's been with the show, the production

Above: Another indoor 'outdoor' set, the garden from 'Maternal Instinct'.

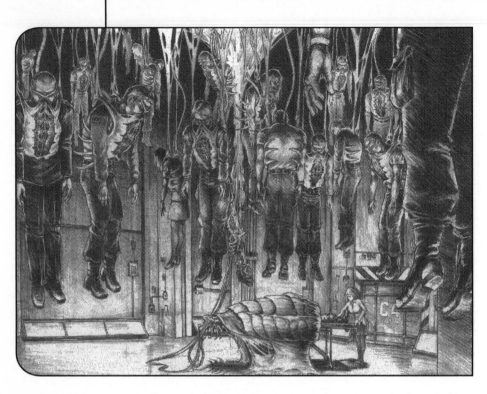

Above: Hanging space in 'Foothold'.

team has never been in the situation where they've built something spectacular only to find out that it's surplus to requirements. Hudolin shrugs, "Everything is needed but sometimes it's not needed to the extent that was first intended. When you're spending $300,000 on a set, you want to be in there for more than a day."

One of the favourite sets amongst cast and crew is the village set created for 'Demons'. "That was the first time we'd actually tried what's called an interior for exterior set," McLean reveals. "We were originally looking at going on location, but then we got talking and I wondered what would happen if we used the existing studio space instead. 'Demons' was another example of the crew getting thoroughly immersed in the project and adding little touches that wouldn't be immediately apparent to the viewers at home."

The team is duly proud of the episode 'Maternal Instinct' too. "That was also an interior space made to look like it was outside and was one of our really successful attempts," Hudolin says. Applauding another group's effort, he admits, "Those sets work so well because we combined them with the visual effects. There are one or two big

shots where you have matte painting and the set combined on the screen, and you're convinced that you are really looking at the sky. We also build the set on panels, and we dropped one panel down so that Jim Menard, the director of photography, could light it from one source — like a sun shining — which made the whole thing look totally realistic."

As innovative as they are, the team's efforts are not without the odd setback. For 'Absolute Power', they designed and built a special hi-tech chair that came out into the room. "One guy who had done a lot of work on the chair went to see X-Men and came back spitting, 'They ripped us off!'" Hudolin remembers, though he is at great pains to clarify that sentiment: "Needless to say they hadn't, but it was pretty funny to see an example of how great minds think alike!"

Asked if there's ever been an occasion when they've been given a brief that sounded too far outside the realms of possibility, Hudolin answers with an unequivocal "No! Not in five years. Our guys live up to that old saying: 'We can do the impossible. Miracles take a little longer...'" λ

Above: Original concept art for the alien lifeforms in 'Scorched Earth'.

Visual Effects

N. John Smith

"These guys have got better ideas, and the equipment has improved beyond recognition, so they are prepared to tackle much bigger effects than we had before, and they manage to pull them off in spectacular fashion."

E ver wondered how it is that the team at *Stargate SG-1* can produce jaw-dropping visual effects episode after episode? Visual effects supervisor James Tichenor insists it's because they have the most brilliant and talented group of people to hand: "I don't think we talk about the outside companies that we use as much as we should when we talk about the effects on *Stargate*, but they are the ones who do the work that makes our show so great." Craftsmen and women from effects houses such as GFVX, Rainmaker Digital and Northwest Imaging combine their considerable talents to create the stunning images that have become synonymous with *Stargate SG-1*. Take season three's 'Nemesis' as an example. Tichenor says, "We got nominated for an Emmy for that show, and it was one that I did mainly with a company called Image Engine Design, who are truly brilliant. We did a show in season two called 'Show and Tell' which was pretty successful, but everyone felt like they wanted to see the creatures, the Reetou, more. I remember Robert Cooper, Brad Wright and Jonathan Glassner came to me and said that they really wanted to do 'Nemesis', which would feature a similar enemy, but needed to know the visual effects team could deliver exactly what they wanted. The concern was that we would have to cut away from the creatures, as we had done with 'Show and Tell', and they wanted to make sure we could have lots and lots of shots of these new bug things, the Replicators." Tichenor grins, "Not knowing whether we could do it or not, I nonchalantly said, 'Yes' and the guys on the team just fell in with me and went for it. I had a pretty decent budget in place, so I talked to Image Engine and told them what was coming and they seemed fairly keen to throw themselves into the madness. In fact, the show was so big every effects house in town, including GVFX and Rainmaker, had a hand in it!"

Tichenor admits that it was one of those situations where working on the episode was a joy and a nightmare at one and the same time: "I felt every kind of emotion you could go through during that show. Most of it was really good, but the stuff I didn't feel so great

about was the whole space walk sequence." He also confesses that it was one of the very few times when he has actually tried to dissuade the producers away from a particular course of action. "I mean, come on, we already had all these spaceships in there, and the ship that crashes into the ocean, and all of the Replicator creatures, *and* the Asgard. This is a forty-five minute television show, not a major feature film! We had all of that stuff and then on top of it, they want a space walk. I told them, 'You know, guys, I think this is pushing it. I don't think we can do this.' But they were all so excited about the idea they said, 'We can do it!' Robert Cooper eventually convinced us and it turned out amazingly well."

The effects supervisor is keen to give credit to all the other artists involved in creating the space walk scene. "A lot of different things went into that sequence that weren't necessarily visual effects. Jim Menard, the director of photography, came up with a system whereby, rather than getting into wires and harnesses and the like, they were able to shoot the actor on a crane, so that it looked like he was float-

Above: The original concept art for a complex VFX scene from 'Nemesis', featuring the Replicants.

ing. Then a combination of human elements and computer graphics elements blended to make the exterior shots of the space ship so effective." However, amongst all these major league effects, Tichenor has a particular fondness for something that was fairly small in the grand scheme of things: the screens on the interior of Thor's ship. "We did these great full wall screens, and I really liked those a lot. Jeremy Howey in our office designed and built the graphics, and then the gang in effects composited them. It's a small thing but I always have a little smile about how well they turned out."

Whilst it may have been a bundle of joy most of the time, Tichenor maintains the hardest shot of all was "crashing the ship into the ocean. It was just so ambitious that I felt we bit off a little more than we could chew there. We decided we were going to do the whole thing in CG and we came up with a really nice ocean, but the actual crash part was stretched to the limit."

Immensely proud of the spectacular effects achieved by his team, Tichenor appears modest in the extreme about the results they manage to pull off. "'Deadman's Switch' wasn't half bad," he offers when

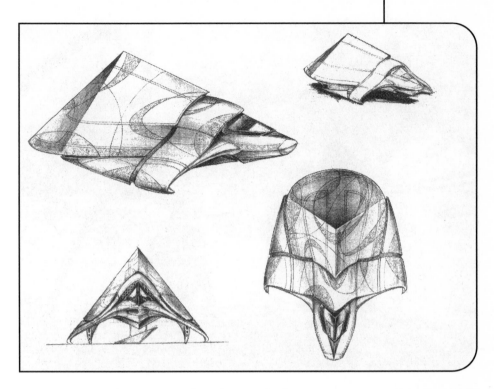

asked to suggest a favourite episode. "That was the first time we ever saw the infamous cargo ship. That was the first complete show I had ever done with Image Engine and it was the test show to see what they could do for us. John Gajdecki [visual effects supervisor for the first two seasons of *Stargate* and Tichenor's mentor] had worked with them on a couple of shots the year before, but that was the first time they really 'went for it', and they came off in spades. Their ability to 'light' CG elements so that they look like they're really in the scene is quite exceptional, and their work with the cargo ship is what convinced us we could do something as adventurous as 'Nemesis' with them later on down the line."

Above: The original concept drawing for the cargo ship, first seen in 'Deadman's Switch', and then in several subsequent episodes.

'Deadman's Switch' was another one of the times when Tichenor had felt that perhaps the desire to do a scene was greater than the capability. He laughs, "The funny thing with that was when we were first storyboarding the episode. Martin Wood, the director, wanted to do this very funky and esoteric way of getting the space ship to look like it was hovering behind the cliffside. He wanted to do this thing where we put one camera on a dolly and then used the camera dolly-

Above: Sam and Thor look out on The O'Neill *in the Emmy-nominated 'Small Victories'.*

ing up to simulate the rise. Then he wanted to shoot an element of Aris Boch just in the window of the ship. His idea was to take that, put it into CG, mirror it and then add footage from a real stationary camera to make it look like the space ship is actually rising with the real guy on the inside of the ship." Wood's initial pitch was not met with unbounded enthusiasm from the visual effects supervisor. In fact he claims, "I went, 'What? That's never gonna work. I don't think it *could* work. I think this is a bad idea. It's going to look weird.' Then Robert Cooper took me aside and gently pointed out, 'You know, when a director has a vision, you don't say no! You just humour him and go for it.'" Tichenor is glad they did because he feels the shot came out "really well."

Beginning and ending season three with nominations for prestigious Gemini and Emmy awards, Tichenor is delighted that season three opener 'Into the Fire' was one of those included in the prestigious accolades. "That was the first episode I did after John Gajdecki left. He started the show, and I was delighted they asked me to take over as head supervisor. That episode was a nice way to start because there were a lot of different bits and pieces, like the ships and the Stargates and the shields, the

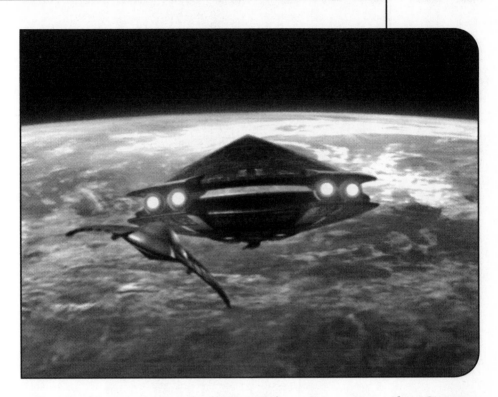

Above: *Outer space action in 'Exodus'.*

explosions and the matte paintings done by Kent Matheson. It was a great little mixture. We got nominated for a Gemini award for that one."

Although Tichenor and the visual effects gang have been nominated for awards ten times, they have actually only walked away with one coveted trophy. "Simon Lacey was honoured by England's Cult TV people and was awarded a place in their Visual Effects Hall of Fame at their Cult Telly Weekend in Liverpool. Needless to say we are all thrilled. Never mind those other ones — this was voted for by the audience who actually watches our show. This was the best award to have won."

Gongs or no gongs, Tichenor maintains that there were so many great episodes in season four that to single out any for special mention as far as visual effects is concerned is remarkably difficult. "'Small Victories' was one of the best shows, again because of the Replicators and the submarine and all those other elements. I think it's the best for pure action. It's got great pace and really flies. It got nominated for an Emmy. In 'Exodus', I got to work with David Warry-Smith again which is always a great experience." The episode that really sticks in

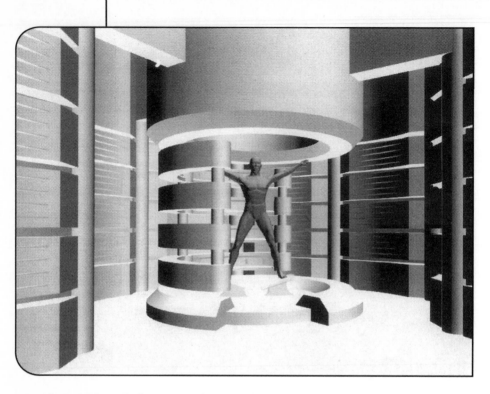

Above: A CGI concept sketch of Lotan's chamber in 'Scorched Earth'.

Tichenor's mind is 'Scorched Earth'. "It's very special to me, because I got to go to Ireland to do the effects for that." Sighing that he didn't get to see a lot of Dublin whilst he was there, he says, "I went for two weeks and only got out once. But going out wasn't why I was there, unfortunately!" The reason Tichenor got to go was because "one of our main guys, Matthew Talbot Kelly, who had been a part of *Stargate SG-1* since season one, working as a compositor between GVFX and Northwest Imaging, had moved to work for Windmill Lane in Ireland. We had always talked about working together again, even if he was across the seas. When 'Scorched Earth' came along, its post-production schedule bridged our hiatus, and because I had worked so hard for the whole of the season I thought, 'Boy! I've gotta get out of here.' Unfortunately there was no way I was going to be able to take time off work during the hiatus because I had to deliver this show on time. I managed to convince the executive producers to let me take the episode to Ireland, so that I could be away from the studios but still do the job. It actually gave us a chance to show that we can do effects all over the world. The guys at Windmill Lane put their hearts and

souls into the episode, and proved that great visual effects artists can work anywhere."

Tichenor says that there were so many innovative visual effects created for 'Scorched Earth', it's difficult to pin point one in particular, but, "I loved the alien hologram they created. Again, you get a new artist and the whole way of looking at things changes. Also the destruction sequence where the ship moves slowly toward the village was completely CG. There are no real elements in there at all. The technology to do that kind of paint FX was literally a couple of months old, so Ronan, the poor guy who did the work, was learning the process as he went along! Right from the terraforming of the planet to the glimpse of the alien ship through the Stargate, that has to be my favourite episode for visual effects."

Concluding that season four was a pretty eventful year, Tichenor says the main thought he'll retain is, "I'm the luckiest man alive. I get to work with an amazing bunch of people, Michelle, Jean-Luc, Steve, Jeremy, Shannon, Kirsten, Neil... for me to sit and be the one that gets all the glory is pretty neat." *Λ*

Above: The effects artists at Ireland's Windmill Lane created this stunning effect for the aptly titled 'Scorched Earth'.

Costume Design

Brad Wright

"I'm extremely proud of the way Christina McQuarrie and her crew continue to create a look that entirely compliments the sentiment of our episodes."

Christina McQuarrie and her team have made literally thousands of costumes for the series over the years, each one playing a part in providing that special quality that makes *Stargate SG-1* stand out from any other science fiction show. Ever modest, the costume designer states, "There is no one particular way to go about creating that otherworldly look, but each script does give us a place to start, and then we always supplement that base with some historical reference. The writers try to give us scripts a few weeks in advance, because even the simplest looking garment takes a bit of thought and preparation, but we're proud of the fact that we complete each show in seven days. Of course, it's all a huge team effort, so the art department influences what we do in terms of matching with their sets, and we do our best to complement the make-up that's being used also."

In the episode 'Fair Game', McQuarrie had to incorporate Roman, East Indian and Chinese flavours into a late twentieth century setting. "We had Cronus, of course, who wears gladiatorial-style garb, alongside Yu — his costume evolved from ancient Chinese garb. Then our Hindu goddess, Nirrti, was based on historical and recent versions of the saris worn by East Asian women for centuries. It was a lot of fun incorporating them into our ultramodern environment. Somehow the mish-mash seems to work!"

Believing that variety is the spice of life, the costume design team take elements from whichever culture is represented in the script and blend them in an unexpected way, often throwing in the odd element from an entirely different culture just to keep the overall look slightly off balance. The fact that the *Stargate* universe is made up of a motley collection of displaced persons helps this along. Says McQuarrie, "In the world and in real life, there are so many wonderful materials — wood, straw, plastic, metal — that can be used to augment any basic costume idea and turn it into something entirely wonderful. We combine modern manmade fabrics with designs we have taken from ancient Egyptian documents, for example, and end up with something that is totally appropriate for what we want to achieve."

Charged with inventing a 'never seen before' quality for those who have been transported to the many worlds through the Stargate, McQuarrie claims that often it's her team's wacky sense of humour that brings an idea to the fore. "When we created the ceremonial head-dress for the Sha're/Ammonet character, the little snake head on her crown was really quite a frivolous notion, but it added that extra something to the overall effect."

There have been many examples of costumes that have enthralled the designers as much as the audience. McQuarrie cites the Red Guard from 'Jolinar's Memories'/'The Devil You Know' arc as her favourite piece: "He wasn't even one of the main characters, he was very much in the background, but he was so wonderful we ended up using him many times. I also love the way we dressed Anna Louise Plowman as Osiris in 'The Curse'. She does appear in more episodes later and we've developed her costumes along a similar theme, but the first time we see her she is in an Earth-based dress that was a flowing, white suit affair. My favourite incidental piece is an amazing Egyptian-style necklace we created to give that kind of flavour to her outfit." ʎ

Opposite page:
The original costume
design for Nirrti.
Above: *Designs for*
Tanith (left) and Yu.

Locations

Jonathan Glassner

"Lynn Smith can come up with the most fantastic locations at the drop of a hat."

Most of the cast or production crew of *Stargate SG-1* wouldn't have a clue where in Vancouver and its environs you could hide a stolen Goa'uld cargo ship. Nor would they know the most likely spot to find a buried Stargate. But they know a woman who does. Location manager Lynn Smith has been searching for the perfect places for location filming (which is any time the production leaves the Bridge Road Studios in Burnaby, British Columbia), since the start of the show's second season. It might not be the most exact science in the universe, but Smith wouldn't trade her job for any number of worlds: "I've never been with a group of people who are so committed to helping each other. That makes a huge difference when you're trying to work miracles every day." Need to find a deep pit to build a military camp in? No problem. Smith found Red Rock Quarry in Port Coquitlam, then the production designers and set builders joined in to create the Stargate buried in the rock for season three's 'New Ground'.

The great 'scout' usually begins when Smith and her assistant Jamie Lake are handed the script, then it's a race against time to come up with the goods: "We start by reading the script a couple of times to get familiar with the story, and the kinds of venues that might be required." Smith and Lake then begin the search for the most suitable location. "We've been doing *Stargate* for some time now," Smith points out, "and hold a lot of information on all the places we've visited over the years." Sometimes it's as simple as returning to an old haunt — Daniel Jackson's apartment for example — but at other times it can mean phoning round

other location managers and their assistants for inspiration. "In the case of personal accommodation for instance, there are agencies which provide information on owners who would like to volunteer their homes, or buildings or whatever. Of course they do get paid quite handsomely, and we do take great care to make sure their property sustains no damage!" Sam Carter's home in season five's 'Ascension' was found in this way.

Smith also credits the writers, saying, "Sometimes they will write a script with a particular place in mind," such as the Observatory in Vancouver's Queen Elizabeth Park, which was used in season two's 'The Gamekeeper' because Jonathan Glassner had brunch there one weekend, and thought it would make a great place to film. Acknowledging the team effort once again, Smith explains, "Sometimes we find a venue which is not quite what the writer or the director is looking for and that's when our production design team and the art department led by Bridget McGuire come into their own. They come along and dress the place with all kinds of things, including trees. [Believe it or not trees were actually added to the scenery for 'Deadman's Switch'.] By the time they are finished the place is totally transformed."

Although the good folk at *Stargate SG-1* can change one of Lynn's locations into whatever the writer/director requires, there is one thing over which no one has any control. "The weather! It can be a major problem and you can't always rely on the weatherman to get it right," Smith laments. During the filming of 'A Hundred Days' (shot on the set built for the television Western *Bordertown*), the climate veered from dense fog to bright sunshine in the course of a single morning, throwing the filming schedule into disarray. Ever cheerful, Smith smiles, "It can cause 'a little disruption', but we usually manage to work it all out." ʎ

Opposite page: The rock-encased Stargate in 'New Ground'.
Above: *Filming 'A Hundred Days', on location at the outdoor set for the TV series* Bordertown.

Stargate and the Fans

Joe Mallozzi

"The ians are so important. I check out the boards on the Internet and keep in touch."

A Report from Gatecon 2001
By Richard Pasco

A s you are no doubt aware (you're reading this book, after all), *Stargate SG-1* enjoys a huge fan following, which seems to have built and built as each year has passed since its début in 1997. Certainly by the end of the fourth season, events to celebrate the show's phenomenal appeal were taking place all across the globe. In the UK, Wolf Events organised the highly successful and entertaining *SG-2*, which was attended by many of the cast, whilst some of those who didn't manage to make it to London did wend their way across to the *Best of Both Worlds* event in Sydney, Australia. Then, the success of 2000's first annual *Gatecon* in the show's hometown encouraged the organisers to do the whole thing once again in September 2001.

The place: Vancouver, Canada. Fans of *Stargate SG-1* are arriving from all corners of the globe, battling against airline chaos following the recent terror attacks in the United States. Despite an overwhelming sense of shock at the atrocities, people are determined to continue with some semblance of normality. Attendees this year have come from as far afield as the United States, England, France, Germany, Spain, Switzerland, Holland, Denmark, Finland, Israel, Saudi Arabia, Japan, Australia and New Zealand.

The venue is the Best Western Convention Center in Richmond, which has been completely taken over by the second annual *SG-1* convention staged by four fans of the show, 'the C4'. While it's true that I am one of those organisers, I'm not writing this as an excuse to say what a great job we did! This is in fact the ideal opportunity to sing the praises of the many other people, all volunteers, who gave up their time and offered their expertise to help make *Gatecon* 2001 such a resounding success. After all, without their input the convention would not have happened.

The action-packed weekend begins on Wednesday 18 September with an organised bus tour of Vancouver, taking in many of the filming locations used in the show. This is an all-day event and proves to be extremely popular — in fact a second tour has to be arranged for the following week to cater for the demand. That same evening an attendee-

organised party takes place at Planet Hollywood, providing a great opportunity for fellow fans to meet up whilst raising money for charity.

Thursday is the main registration day when the convention-goers get their first glimpse of the 100 or so items donated to the charity auction. The collection includes many items given by Stargate Productions, with articles of cast clothing and replica props taking centre stage.

The dealers' room also opens its doors today, and includes the first public outing for the official *Stargate SG-1* Fan Club. Also present are dealers from Australia, Canada and the States, and Don S. Davis selling some of his original artwork. Then there's the United States Air Force stand, and finally the *Gatecon* table, selling convention merchandise and a range of brand new official *Stargate* items. That evening the first event takes place, in the form of an informal cocktail party with special guest Alexis Cruz (Skaara), attending his first ever convention. He proves to be very popular, and spends his evening moving from table to table, chatting with everyone present.

Friday sees the start of the convention proper, and as attendees file into the main room there are gasps of astonishment as they see the fantastic stage constructed by Stargate Productions, which gives the impression of a Goa'uld mothership, complete with gold hieroglyphs and braziers. Covering the centre stage is a black cloth, which then drops with

Above: Two guests enjoying Gatecon 2001: N. John Smith (co-executive producer, left) and Jay Acovone (Major Charles Kawalsky).

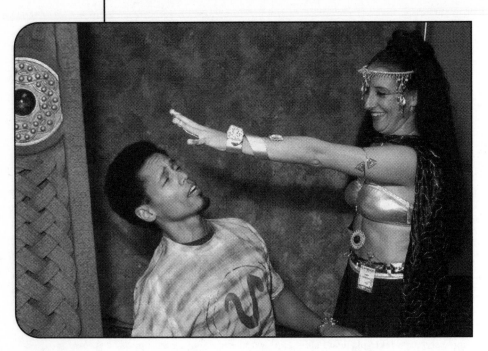

Above: Peter Williams (Apophis) gets a dose of his own medicine.

a flourish to reveal a ten-foot high replica of the Stargate itself, set against a glittering star field. After a minute's silence in recognition of those who lost their lives in New York and Washington, the show kicks into action with the ever-popular music videos, as images and video clips of past convention action fill the twin screens.

During the course of the day fans are treated to question and answer sessions with Alexis Cruz, Tony Amendola, Jay Brazeau, Jay Acovone and JR Bourne, plus a guest appearance by Virginia Hey from *Farscape*, another immensely popular sci-fi show. On Saturday the stage also plays host to Don S. Davis, Gary Jones, Peter Williams, Peter DeLuise, Peter Woeste, William Gereghty, Martin Wood, Andy Mikita, Colin Cunningham and Teryl Rothery, many of whom also take part in the hugely popular photograph sessions. The convention's main surprise guest is revealed when Amanda Tapping appears, spending an hour on stage chatting with the assembled throng. In the evening, following a well supported costume contest, comes possibly the highlight of the whole weekend — the charity auction, held once again to raise money for the *Make a Wish Foundation*. After a moving speech from wish child Tara Mitrovic, who tells how her dog Boomer appeared in an episode of the show as part of her wish, the action

begins. Hosted by the actors, item after item is put up for grabs, as the fans' fervour is unleashed in a bidding frenzy. The most expensive item of the evening is a crystal skull, from the episode of the same name, which attains a winning bid of $2,400!

Sunday morning dawns with steaming credit cards still recovering from the night before. Whilst forty lucky winners of a draw get to spend an hour touring the *Stargate* studios, guests on stage back at the convention include Dan Shea, Brad Wright, John Smith, Robert Cooper, Paul Mullie and Joseph Mallozzi, plus the main cast's stand-ins. The convention also makes it onto national Canadian television, as a cameraman from *Inside Entertainment* records the day's events. Meanwhile, attendees are able to take part in autograph sessions, which provide the ideal opportunity to meet and chat with their favourite actors.

Gatecon 2001 has grown to cover a period of six days, if you include the two city tour days, and many attendees make it their main holiday of the year. It's a chance to meet up with old friends from previous conventions, and to forge new friendships with like-minded people who share the same love and appreciation for that most exciting, innovative and well-produced of shows — *Stargate SG-1*. Here's to next year... ⋏

Above: Jay Acovone, Peter Williams, Tony Amendola (Bra'tac), and Don S. Davis (Hammond) give a special performance of a fan's SG-1 story.

Afterword

ell, anyone can write a Foreword. It's long forgotten by the time you reach the end of the book. The Afterword is where the last impression is formed. It's where the whole experience of reading the book is punctuated. In fact, you could say it's the most important part of the book. Obviously, I felt the pressure all those who have written Afterwords have felt before me. Thankfully, I thought back to a suggestion I once read in one of those books called *How to Write a Screenplay in Three Days* or something like that: always consider your audience. I figure there are two types of people reading this right now. Either you are such a passionate, devoted fan of *Stargate SG-1* that you have read all the way through this whole book, or you work on the show and you're checking to see if I mention you kindly.

To the first group, thank you. Thank you for liking what we do, not only enough to watch the show, but enough to read a book about it all the way to the end. The cynics among you might think us television writer/producers are just money hungry sell-outs who would write anything for a buck and that may be true, but believe me, in this case, *SG-1* is not anything. I know I speak for everyone who works on the show when I say we all desperately want it to be great. We may not always succeed, but we try our very best all the time. The fact that there are those of you who like *SG-1* enough to call yourselves fans honestly makes us quite giddy. So, thank you. Thank you for knowing the difference between a Goa'uld and a Jaffa. For knowing "Selmak on the Peltac of a Teltac heading for Delmak" wasn't written by Dr Seuss. For loving Martouf so damn much. For knowing Harsesis is not a dermatological condition. For being both shippers and non-shippers. For understanding that two-way travel through a wormhole is scientifically unsound. For getting excited by the phrase "unscheduled off-world activa-

tion". And most of all, thank you for watching. May your Seventh Chevron always lock.

Now, as for the other people, those of you skimming for your name — singling people out is always such a dangerous game, isn't it? Someone's always going to feel slighted. Oh well, I guess I'd rather piss off a few people than not mention the following. First of all, thanks to Thomasina for writing this book and being as devoted a fan as anyone paid tribute to above. Jonathan, thanks for teaching me and for becoming a friend, and despite the fact that I do miss you, thanks for leaving — they gave me your office. Joe, Paul, Peter, Martin, thanks for making it fun to come to work every day. You guys are the first audience for whom I write. If you like it, I'm happy. I know I've got gold if Joe cries. Granted it hasn't happened yet, but that's why I signed on for season six. Michael, thinking back over the five years we've worked together I realised you've made me a better writer.

One day, you really will have no notes. Until then, I will strive to reach your expectations. Brad, I hope you know how I feel about you, man. You quite simply changed my life. In a very good way. There are so many more people up whose butts I have not blown smoke, but honestly it's not my fault, I was given a maximum word limit. So, Hank, John, Rick, John, Amanda, John, Chris, John, Don, John, Cath-Anne, John, Jim, John, James, John, Peter W., John (we have a lot of Johns), Mark, Steve (I think there's a Steve) and of course, who could forget Andy — to all of you, named and unnamed, there will never be another show like it, until the spin-off, and there will never be a better group of people to work with, unless I work with all of you again. I should be so lucky.

*Opposite page: Dialling home. **Above:** Robert C. Cooper.*

Robert C. Cooper
Executive Producer *Stargate SG-1*

Below: Thomasina Gibson visiting the Gateroom set.

Thomasina Gibson trained as a schoolteacher, but decided to develop her love of theatre by moving to Stratford upon Avon, working at the Royal Shakespeare Theatre for several seasons, until the travel bug bit. She embarked on a career with British Airways Long Haul division — a move that took her to almost every corner of the Globe — although the Falklands and Antarctica are still on her list of places to visit. Three years at the BBC followed, where Gibson was part of a team of four that co-produced and presented a mid-morning sequence programme on Radio Sussex, was production assistant to the Arts and Youth programmes Producer and contributed news and entertainment segments to BBC Television's *South Today*. Having taken a long break to raise two children, she returned to writing initially as a hobby, and now writes for the majority of film and television magazines in the UK and several printed and on-line publications in the United States. Aside from sci-fi, she has contributed arts and sports features to the *Daily Telegraph* newspaper. A huge fan of cult television, she has worked as a consultant on several sci-fi/cult related shows, including the BBC's *Lost in Space* series and Channel 4's factual documentary *Riddle of the Skies*, and is proud to have worked as an associate producer on several 'added value' reports for MGM's *Stargate SG-1* DVDs. A young person's sci-fi series, *Dark Side of the Sun*, which Gibson co-wrote with Terry James (*Tess of the D'Urbevilles*, *Children of the New Forest*), is due to go into production in 2002. **λ**